Relevance in the Workplace

Using the Bible to Impact Your Job

By

Gary Blackard

Intermedia Publishing Group

Relevance in the Workplace
Using the Bible to Impact Your Job

Published by:
Intermedia Publishing Group, Inc.
P.O. Box 2825
Peoria, Arizona 85380
www.intermedia pub.com

ISBN 978-1-935906-38-4

Acknowledgements

I am truly a blessed man and have had many family, friends and colleagues support me throughout my career. First and foremost, I want to thank my parents, Bill and Faith Blackard, who raised my sister and I in a loving home, surrounded by prayer and engaged in the Word of God. My dad was the first to model living out your faith at work in my life. My mom's prayers have a direct line to the throne room and have saved me on more than one occasion I am sure.

I also want to thank Ron Henry, President of the Sterling Group, but more importantly mentor and friend. Ron, you'll never know how much our Starbucks meetings impacted me. Thank you to Stephen Christensen, Jeff Gore, Cathy Fletcher, and Danny Ruiz who were the original board members for Eagle Peak Leadership. Their friendship and support means so much to me.

To Terry Whalin, thank you so much for leading me through the publishing process.

Special thanks to Danny Ruiz, Hezekiah Barge and Jordan Hansen. These three men have had tremendous influence in my life and I appreciate their prayers, their advice and their camaraderie.

Finally, I need to thank my wife, Debra, and my two children, Joseph and Crystal. They spent many nights without their husband/father in the last several years due to business travel requirements. This book is a testimony to their sacrifice.

Dedication

To my wife, Debra Ann, who sacrificed much during many miles I was on the road.

I love you deeply.

Table of Contents

Chapter 1

Viewing Work a Different Way

A few summers ago, I had arrived in Asia (specific details are not given for confidentiality reasons) tired from a thirteen plus hour United flight. I was in Asia on a four city, three country business trip visiting several high profile customers. After arriving at the JW Marriott, I settled into my room and travel habits. Part of my daily activities (a better definition may be discipline—more on this later) is to pray for the next day's business activities asking for God to use me for His Glory, help me to perform well, and to give me wisdom in my business—this is not easy sometimes and I fail at times to truly give it my all. When morning came, I met with one of the local managers who had agreed to transport me to the customer location for a site tour and customer meeting. As we proceeded to the client location, the manager and I had the opportunity to discuss several topics including life in general and differences between our countries. I immediately prayed (silently of course) that if I "opened the door" with a "Christian" statement then He would have to "open the opportunity" to share directly. I proceeded to make a statement about persecution stories (persecution of churches, etc.) I had heard about and asked for this manager's opinion. This statement led to a thirty-five minute discussion around Christianity and what it means to have a relationship with God. I was privileged to lead the manager to accept Christ as Lord in the basement parking lot of the customer's location. One of my favorite memories is watching this manager as they folded hands (in the traditional way) and echoed the words of my prayer. We went on to have an outstanding customer meeting and operational review.

There are several things to learn from this. First of all, this is a byproduct of integrating Faith and Work. Opportunities like this seldom happen "on a whim" and God expects us to always be open and available, living out our lives (including work) as examples first. The second point is that I would have never had this opportunity had I not performed my job to the best of my abilities enabling me to travel internationally. Francis Schaeffer, a noted Christian Philosopher, stated, "If you do your work well, you will have a chance to speak."[1] I firmly believe this and have witnessed its truth in my own life and in the lives of other Christians successfully integrating their Faith and Work. Thirdly, there are many other ways (besides verbally witnessing about the Gospel) a Christian can successfully practice Marketplace Christianity. The Bible is filled with wisdom for all markets, in all industries and for jobs of every kind. This book will help explore this. But first, what is all this talk about Faith and Work? My mother would say that it is somewhat a shame that we have to create ministries to help Christians integrate their faith at work when this should be a natural occurrence as each Christian grows in his or her walk. There is a lot of truth to this. Unfortunately, we live in a day and age where compromise is rampant and false assumptions are made. Because of this, we need ministries to focus Christians on living out the biblical worldview in all areas of their lives, including the workplace.

The Faith at Work movement has been intermittent at best over the last one hundred years. There are many organizations devoted to marketplace ministries throughout the world; however, much more is needed to truly understand how Faith[2] has and can positively impact the workplace or marketplace in general. Scholars, like David Miller (Yale and Princeton Universities), have completed new research on the subject (his book *God at Work* is an outstanding work on the history of the faith and work movement[3]) and churches along with individuals are beginning to recognize the need for tools and methodologies to develop their own integration of faith and work. However, it's not only Christianity that is seeing this trend. Recent books by New Age groups such as *God goes to Work* and Buddhism groups such as *Buddha: 9 to 5* have been written to speak to improving the workplace.

The argument for the positive integration/relationship of faith and work is nothing new. Though some critics disagree with portions of his theory, Max Weber defined this relationship in his book *The Protestant Ethic and the Spirit of Capitalism.*[4] According to an author on Wikipedia, "Weber shows that certain types of Protestantism favored rational pursuit of economic gain and that worldly activities had been given positive spiritual and moral meaning. It was not the goal of those religious ideas, but rather a byproduct—the inherent logic of those doctrines and the advice based upon them both directly and indirectly encouraged planning and self-denial in the pursuit of economic gain."[5] Whether you agree or disagree with the tenets of Weber's theory, one would find it very difficult to disprove that Protestantism has had a positive impact on the economy. Martin Luther also expressed the value of one's work as God's calling. If Christianity has had a positive influence, then why segregate it? After years of maintaining this private/public dualism, it seems that Corporate America is beginning to open its doors to the realization that faith and work can and should be integrated together.

There has been a slow shift emerging over the last fifty years in Corporate America regarding the acceptance of workplace spirituality. However, in the last twenty years, this shift has accelerated and we are seeing many books, articles and non-profits all specializing or communicating about workplace spirituality. For example, in many companies we are now seeing the use of corporate chaplains as an added benefit for their workforce—"Corporate Chaplains of America" is a non-profit in this area. Academia has also seen unprecedented growth in the integration of faith and work. Many universities offer specialized courses in workplace religion and how to integrate spirituality in the workplace.[6] Universities offering these courses include Harvard Business School, Yale Business School, and many others across the United States and in other parts of the world.

There is significant interest in the integration of faith and work in many different industries including the government and military. Just this week, I received a *Connected* newsletter that the Officer's Christian Fellowship puts out monthly. In the letter from the Interim Director (a retired U.S. Army Colonel), he speaks about the integration of faith and profession stating, "the key thought here is integral, whole or complete, our desire to be the same person with the same motivations in every aspect of our lives. That wholeness will be characterized by servant leadership, selfless service, compassion, and love for all—and our witness will be primarily through our professional excellence."[7]

Why are we seeing this growth in the interest of workplace spirituality? One common theme seems to arise from most of the writings and that is the recognition that we can no longer separate our lives into public and private spheres. Author and one of the UK's leading thinkers on employment, Richard Donkin writes, "Social attitudes and value systems have always been integral to our relationship with work. It is vital that employers understand this if they are to build businesses that are embodied in the people who work for the company. Moreover, work can no longer be divorced from life as a separate entity, something that is left behind when we leave the office or factory gate. Nor does it make sense that we should seek some kind of work-life balance. This jaded concept presents work and life as two distinct experiences. They are not. We don't stop living when we go to work and, very often today, we don't stop working when we arrive home."[8] HSBC Chairman Stephen Green writes, "Compartmentalization—dividing life up into different realms, with different ends and subject to different rules—is a besetting sin of human beings... One of the most obvious and commonplace manifestations of the tendency to compartmentalize is seeing our work life as being a neutral realm in which questions of value (other than shareholder value) or of rightness (other than what is lawful) or of wisdom (other than what is practical) need not arise."[9] From another business executive's perspective, I believe another major reason is that people are either unaware of how to integrate their faith at work (but have grown tired of segregating them) or are ignorant of the relevance the Bible has for the workplace. I have managed hundreds of employees in my career and have heard common themes when discussing their career paths or personal goals. They want to better understand their purpose of why they are doing what they are doing besides bringing home a paycheck to pay the bills.

Author Gary Hamel in his book *The Future of Management* [10] writes of the need for future managers to understand meaning and purpose in their jobs and careers as they balance their religious beliefs and their development. Author and Wharton Business Management Professor Stewart Friedman writes, "In my research and coaching work over the past two decades, I have met many people who feel unfulfilled, overwhelmed, or stagnant because they are forsaking performance in one or more aspects of their lives. They aren't bringing their leadership abilities to bear in all of life's domains—work, home, community, and self (mind, body, and spirit). Of course, there will always be some tension among the different roles we play. But, contrary to the common wisdom, there's no reason to assume that it's a zero-sum game. It makes more sense to pursue excellent performance as a leader in all four domains-achieving what I call 'four-way wins'—not trading off one for another but finding mutual value among them."[11] Miroslav Volf, Director for the Yale Center for Faith and Culture, stated "When the meaning of work is reduced to the well-being of the working self, the result is a feeling of melancholy and unfulfillment, even in the midst of apparent success."[12] It is crucial that business managers and leaders feel a sense of purpose and meaning in their careers. Simply ignoring this under-developed need can and will negatively impact job performance, productivity, retention rates, customer loyalty and satisfaction, and bottom line profits. Churches unfortunately have failed in meeting this need as well. Many pastors today do not relate to what their congregants are going through at work and so inadvertently avoid preaching on subjects that can impact the marketplace. Economist Jay Richards recognized this. He writes, "Churchgoing business people endure sermons that show little understanding of business."[13]

That being said, there is also much more to the integration of faith and work than defining the purpose of our jobs/careers, or building integrity on the job through biblical principles of honesty, servanthood, and good conduct. The thesis of this writing is that Christianity and its sacred text, The Holy Bible, can impact performance in the marketplace in all areas across all industries and cultures. Business professionals, tradesmen, homemakers, public servants, healthcare workers, and countless other careers can all benefit from what the Bible teaches about areas of the marketplace. These areas include (though not inclusive) customer experience, strategy, continuous improvement, finance and stewardship, sustainability, leadership, marketing and human capital management.

I write this from a business perspective having many years of experience in Corporate America and with Fortune 100 companies all over the world. I have had the privilege of traveling to many countries and working with various global business organizations. All too often we see authors and speakers in the workplace movement who have very little secular work experience (or who have not taken the time and energy to learn what others are facing), or they are full-time ministers/evangelists, in full-time academia or non-profit positions. While there is certainly nothing wrong with this in general, sometimes the lack of secular business or work experience minimizes the effectiveness on teaching other people who work in everyday secular jobs or careers. There is also a credibility gap that can become a barrier to learning.

For example, business professionals face different time constraints, stresses and situations than do ministers or professors. People associate experience with knowledge and rightly so. Though one can gain academic/educational knowledge in various areas of the workplace without empirical or experiential knowledge in these same areas, one cannot fully understand the workplace area without experiencing it first hand. I can learn about Firefighting through education, the media, and interviewing Firefighters. However, I cannot say I fully understand firefighting as I have never carried hose up flights of stairs, nor have I given CPR to someone, nor have I sprayed water on a fire. Even further, I cannot fully understand the political, social and cultural differences that take place in a fire station or department on any given day and/or in any given city.

Another example between business professionals and ministers would be time constraint differences for spiritual reflection or spiritual disciplines (Bible reading, prayer, solitude, etc.). Typically (as it should be), ministers have dedicated time for such activities during their work schedules to ensure they are fully meeting the requirements of their positions. Most business professionals have to schedule time for spiritual disciplines outside of their work schedule for many different reasons including workload. I use this as an example because I had the privilege of speaking to a group of young business professionals in Guangzhou, China about the balance of God and Work. Their feedback to me was they had heard from their respective pastors on making time for God; however, due to my business experience and successes, they felt I understood more where they were coming from and could show them examples within their own careers. My intent here is not to belittle the awesome privilege and responsibility of full-time paid (we are all in full-time ministry if you really think about it) ministry nor is it to boast of my experience, only to show the different perspectives from various backgrounds and experiences. Though it is good that others are willing to discuss workplace ministry, we also need to hear from Christians directly employed in the marketplace and how they are integrating their Faith in their careers and workplaces and what value it brings both to them and to their jobs.

I also write this as a Christian who has witnessed the awesome effects of God's Word on the marketplace. I have spoken with many Christians in Asia, Europe and North America gathering their input on the integration of their faith with the workplace. Most importantly, I have seen the changes that God has brought to the lives of these Christians around the world and in my own life and career, all through the knowledge of the Holy.[14] I remember speaking at a university gathering in China and towards the end of the Q&A period, a young Chinese woman asked me how to handle a manager who was mean to her. I told her that we must live consistently as an example, work to the best of our ability each day, and make it a matter of careful prayer for the manager. I told her and the rest of the hundred plus students to never underestimate the power of prayer in any area of your life, including work. I took down her name and her request in front of the group and promised to pray for her and her manager. I sent emails every few weeks to check in. About three months or so went by when I received a fantastic e-mail. One of my hosts had e-mailed me and said this young woman's manager had completely changed his attitude towards her and was very professional and respectful. That is the power of faith in the workplace.

Another intent of this writing is to show people from different cultures and careers how the Bible can improve your performance on the job thereby improving the marketplace in general. Various tools and methodologies will be discussed throughout this book. They are not meant to be considered the "exclusive" set of tools and methodologies. Years of prayer, research, experience and global travel have yielded these thoughts. My purpose and prayer is that you will read these pages and come to understand how important the Bible is to all areas of life, including the marketplace.

The Value of Work

Have you have felt good after a hard day's work? Your mind and/or your muscles may be tired and sore, but you had a feeling of accomplishment, that you had worked hard and have seen the results. I have had many days like this. There is something to be said about the feeling of accomplishing a task, of doing work. This is especially true of physical labor. I remember taking a group of people from a church where I was the Men's Ministries leader to a ranch where a Christian family had a ministry in hosting youth camps, retreats, etc. Calicento Ranch is one of my favorite places to visit and the Perelli family who owns and runs it is truly a family of God. I had offered volunteer labor to the ranch and labor we did. One of the things needed was a foundation pad to be dug out in the side of a sloping hill. This pad would be used in building a bakery to be used for the ministry. With shovels, gloves and hard work, we dug out that pad. It took the better part of a day to get it done. I remember how sore we all were on the drive back to Orange County where we were from. I remember the dirt, the sweat and the pain and nothing felt better. We had ministered through one of the key areas of life that God has given us: work.

Secular philosophers recognize the value of work as well. Philosopher Matthew Crawford writes, "...indeed, there are fewer occasions for the kind of spiritedness that is called forth when we take things in hand for ourselves, whether to fix them or to make them."[15] Crawford goes on to write about the value of physical, mechanical labor. He deliberately compares to the "knowledge worker" of today and what differences prevail between the two. All moral work has value (There are some occupations where value loosely defined, unethical or criminal in some cases—for example a drug dealer "works" but what value does he bring?) whether physical or mental, blue collar or white collar, public serving or private sector. Philosopher Alain de Botton, in his book entitled *The Pleasures and Sorrows of Work,* writes of several different occupations around the world. He studies the value of the occupation and what the individuals feel when doing the work. One occupation he describes is a Cargo Ship Spotter in London. These workers spend days monitoring ships from the docks and documenting the various stats about them. Botton was so impressed with these workers that he gives them credit for inspiring the writing of his book.[16] He also states how much we might learn from them as they enjoy the intricacies of their work and understanding what cargo is being carried by each ship and where each ship is headed to. Both Crawford and Botton have hit upon something, though nothing new. These two philosophers of today recognized that work, even with its sorrows and trials, when done in proper context, is valuable to the human soul. All throughout history, humanity has recognized the value of work though as the years have turned to centuries, the value of work has been misinterpreted at times and often neglected, especially in the Christian circles. Benjamin Franklin once wrote, "When men are employed they are best contented."[17] William Penn wrote in 1693, "Love Labour: for if thou dost not want it (labor) for food, thou mayest for physic. It (labor) is wholesome for thy body and good for thy mind. It (labor) prevents the fruits of idleness, which many times comes of nothing to do, and leads too many to do what is worse than nothing."[18] I believe William Penn got it right. This is the biblical worldview of work. God designed work for our pleasure and our growth. It came before the fall of man into sin. Work is not a result of sin as God gave work to Adam prior to Adam's disobedience. Work is more than the task at hand and should always be done keeping Christian servanthood to Christ in mind. Let's explore a little deeper what the Bible says about work.

The first mention of work in the Bible besides God's work in creation is found in Genesis. God had created the Garden of Eden, a lush paradise with animals, birds and teeming with plants, fruits and water. Adam was told to *work and keep* the garden.[19] The King James Version translates it as "to dress it and to keep it." The Hebrew word for dress or work is *abad* which means to work, to till, to tend to, to serve. The Hebrew word for keep is *shamar* which means to hedge about, to protect and attend to, to preserve. God instructed Adam to work in the garden with service and protection. Adam was to take care of the garden God had provided for him. Let's apply this to our own jobs and work. Do we look at our work as a provision from God? Do we attend to our jobs as if God has given it to us? I believe that if Christians truly lived by this principle, every corporation, human resources professional, recruiter, and hiring manager would be seeking Christians for employment. They would see the results of living out that principle. If we believe that God is all-powerful, all-knowing and omnipresent, then we know that we are in his care and the job we currently are in is of no surprise to him. God designed business (in the broader term) and we are all part of that design. The sooner we change our attitudes and behaviors towards work and treat it as if God placed us there, the sooner we will find real value. Does this mean you should not worry about promotions or transitioning to new industries? On the contrary, God also designed humanity to be creative, to adapt, to grow and to learn. As we learn new things and grow in our lives, it is only natural to be drawn towards other goals or objectives. The point is that whatever you are *currently* employed in, believe that God has placed you there for a purpose even it is short-lived because he has.

As we progress through the Old and New Testaments, we begin to read about the changes in commerce and how new occupations were being created. Though largely livestock and agriculture ruled the early ages, there were still many different types of work. Artists, musicians, brick layers, shepherds, farmers, soldiers, tax collectors, tentmakers, carpenters, fishermen, government officials, and retail merchants were just some of the jobs mentioned in the Old and New Testaments. Work played a significant part in God's design and therefore in His Word. The seventeenth century preacher, Richard Steele, wrote of God's intention of work when he stated, "…

the Command of Almighty God to all his posterity, is, that six days they should labour and do all their work: in this is plainly implied, that all should fill up their time with some proper employment, from one season of religious rest to another."[20]

There are three principles we can learn from the biblical worldview of work. Principle number one is that God created work. New jobs are being developed every year it seems. I just read in a recent periodical that the top ten in-demand technology jobs of 2009 did not exist in 2004.[21] That is incredible when you think about it. From farmers to the Industrial Age to the Technology Age, to the future, we continue to evolve work and our workplaces. One truth remains. Humanity may be developing new jobs all of the time and will continue to do so but we did not develop work in general. God did.

Principle number two is that God expects us to work. God placed Adam in the garden and commanded him to work and keep it. God did not say if you want to. Or Adam, I know you don't like working, but at least give it a try. No, God told Adam to work in the garden and keep it or care for it. Bill Heatley (IT Director at a large healthcare provider) writes, "From the beginning, work and care have been bonded together under God. The loving nature of God can be seen in its unblemished beginning. In their tending of the garden, Adam and Eve would find purpose and fulfillment."[22] God expects us to work because he knows there is purpose and fulfillment in it because that's the way he designed it. Theologian and Professor David Jensen writes, "Work, as vocation, is fulfilling not because it enriches oneself (though it may), but because of its obedient response to the creator. The value of vocation is not self-referential, but in rendering one's work to God, in all components of one's life."[23] We are primarily fulfilled in work because we are obedient to God. Self enrichment is just a byproduct. The apostle Paul writes regarding work on several occasions throughout his letters that fall under the principle that God expects us to work. Two reasons are for purpose and for fulfillment as we have learned. Paul discusses two other reasons. The first is to be self-reliant and the second is to avoid being a burden and giving someone an opportunity to speak negatively against Christianity. Paul writes to the church in Thessalonica (1 Thess. 4:11-12) to be quiet in their studies, to mind their own business, to work with their own hands. Why? The reason is found in verse twelve. Paul writes, "that ye may walk honestly toward all them that are without, and that ye may have lack of nothing." Paul states that if they kept to themselves and stopped being busybodies and worked with their own hands, they could walk in honest reward and be self-reliant. Paul goes on to write in a second letter to the same church that if a man did not work, he should not eat.[24] This is strong language but Paul understood the commands of God. There are reasons why God expects us to work. Paul and the others traveling with him made it a point to work each day in whatever city they were in so that they might be an example to the church and to have the church follow that example of working hard and being self-reliant and avoiding becoming a burden on others.[25]

The third principle regarding the biblical worldview of work is that God expects us to work as unto His Son, Jesus Christ. Our actions, attitudes and behaviors on the job should be done as if we are doing them for Christ himself. Let that one sink in a moment. I know I have failed to do this on many an occasion. I have made many mistakes in having the wrong attitude or making the wrong decision. Paul writes to the church at Colossae speaking of servants (basically employees), "and whatsoever ye do, do it heartily, *as to the Lord*, and not unto men."[26] This Scripture also is related to Ecclesiastes 9:10 that states whatsoever thy hand findeth to do, do it with all thy might… God expects us to give our best in the workplace because we are working as unto him. Our results are for his glory. Our sales, our reports, our number of cars repaired are all to bring glory to him. That is the number one purpose.

In summary, these three principles can help us change our attitudes and actions towards work. God created work. God expects us to work. God expects us to work as unto his son, Jesus Christ. If we develop our learning centered around these three principles, we will find our purpose and be truly fulfilled no matter what job we find ourselves in. There is value in work and it is such a big part of our lives. We spend approximately 25 to 30 percent of our entire lives working, some much more. We need to change our worldview of work to the biblical worldview of work. Theologian and Professor in Glasgow, Darrell Cosden writes, "A new belief about work will enable us, in the Spirit, to interpret and evaluate our work and ways of working in fresh ways so that our 'sanctified imaginations' can bring forth seeds of change. We will find ourselves envisioning new work and godly ways of doing our work. From this, and to the degree that we have influence where we work, change will begin to take place. Our spirituality will become real to us and we will begin to flourish as God's people."[27] That is my prayer for you and for me. May God grant us a new vision for our work. May he strengthen us to be bold at work. May we work hard giving our best at all we do, as unto him.

In Summary:

What does work mean to you? Be open and honest.

_____

_____

_____

_____

Think about a time when you worked really hard and felt really good about it. Why did it feel so good?

_____

_____

_____

_____

Principle # 1 is that God created work as a benefit. Do you agree or disagree? Why?

_____

_____

_____

_____

Principle # 2 is that God expects us to work. Examine your work life. Do you see the reasons why God expects us to work?

_____

_____

_____

_____

Principle # 3 is that God expects us to work as unto his Son, Jesus Christ. Why is this difficult to grasp?

_____

_____

_____

_____

Read 2 Thessalonians 3:10. What do you think of this verse?

_____

_____

_____

_____

Sample prayer for understanding the value of work:

> *Lord Jesus,*
>
> *Thank you for understanding me. Thank you for the blessing of work. Help me to understand your worldview of work and help me to apply it to my life. Teach me your ways as the Psalmist asks. Let me see work with a fresh, Godly perspective and use me for your glory in my job.*
>
> *Amen.*

Your worldview and its impact on your job and workplace

The day was new and cold and I was seated in the back of one of London's famous black cabs on my way from Heathrow airport to Canary Wharf in London where I was meeting with a global financial services firm. It had been a long flight and I was staring out the foggy windows taking in the scenery, something I do on every business trip. I have learned that you can never take God's creation for granted and you can always learn something if you are willing to observe (a trait picked up from my parents). The highway leading into London is surrounded by green fields, farms, soccer (football) fields, and a mixture of old and new architecture.

As we were driving, I noticed a delivery van that had pulled along side. On the side of the van, a technology company had painted their marketing slogan. It was a picture of the evolutionary cycle from monkey to mankind and the slogan read "Hire intelligence". The obvious meaning to this was that if one hired this company for technology solutions, one would certainly hire a new evolutionary intelligence of course playing on the Darwinian theory of Evolution. But there is more to it than simple marketing. What is being portrayed is a worldview. The assumption with this marketing is that one would believe in the Darwinian theory to apply it to what they are trying to sell. It is not my intention to debate the validity of this theory (there are many other writings and authors much more qualified to speak to this). My intention is simply to show how a worldview can penetrate the business environment.

What is a worldview? One definition is "a worldview comprises one's collection of presuppositions, convictions, and values from which a person tries to understand and make sense of the world and life."[28] A worldview is what we use to interpret life and the application thereof. We each have our own personal worldview and use it in all areas of our life including when we arrive for work in factories, warehouses, stores, offices, departments, on farms and in building sites around the world.

For many years, companies have tried to segregate personal beliefs and worldviews from the workplace. This is impossible to do. Many companies have human resources policies forbidding the display of religious materials even in the confines of the employee's workspace. I have heard it said many times in my career that one's religion or spirituality does not belong in the workplace and can be offensive in nature. Certainly there have been examples where extremism or improper religious discussion has had negative impact. However, I would argue there are much more positive results realized when employees are free to express their worldviews within certain guidelines. More important, I would also argue that employees cannot separate their worldview from their job.

A worldview is defined as "the lens through which someone views the world." For example, if you are an atheist, you have a worldview that God does not exist. As the atheist looks at different areas in life, he or she develops their worldview through this lens. Science becomes the guiding force for most atheists. In the workplace, the atheist may look at customer experience in different ways than other peers such as a Buddhist. Atheists would generally look to facts and "scientific evidence" to improve the customer experience while the Buddhist may focus more on the spiritual impact of improving another's satisfaction. If we look deeper into what drives our worldviews, I believe we would be surprised at how much we interpret through this lens even in the workplace.

One of the most prominent examples of how worldviews impact workplaces, governments, and populations is found in the history of the United States. The eighteenth century saw the birth of a new nation, one founded on a Judeo-Christian worldview. Of course it did not start in the eighteenth century. The foundation was laid at Jamestown, Plymouth and a host of other cities as Puritans, Lutherans, Quakers, Baptists, Presbyterians and other religious folks made their way to Early America in the seventeenth century. We all have studied in History how the Pilgrims pledged that for the glory of God and the advancement of the Christian Faith, they were coming to Virginia to plant a colony. Storms ended up pushing them to Massachusetts but their purpose remained the same: to glorify God and advance the Christian Faith.[29]

With this foundation and the Great Awakening that followed, led by Jonathan Edwards and George Whitefield, America was on a collision course with the destiny God had for it. This did not mean it was not difficult to get there. Many different denominations made up the Judeo-Christian worldview along with varying devotions to differences in doctrine including Calvinism and Armenianism. Harvard Professor Alan Heimert wrote of this in a very detailed book called *Religion and the American Mind: From the Great Awakening to the Revolution.* There were many factions, infighting, and debates on who was right and wrong. What is true, however, is that no matter their differences, most fell under the "Judeo-Christian" umbrella.

On September 7, 1774, Pastor Jacob Duche of the Anglican Church, opened the session of Congress with the reading of Psalm 35 and a prayer. His prayer asked for wisdom in the activities of Congress, preservation of health, justice to be done, and closed with "All this we ask in the name and through the merits of Jesus Christ thy son, Our Saviour, Amen."[30] It sounds like our Founding Fathers knew the value of the integration of faith and work. Jon Meacham writes, "Belief in God is central to the country's experience, yet for the broad center, faith is a matter of choice, not coercion, and the legacy of the Founding is that the sensible center holds. It does so because the Founders believed themselves at work in the service of both God and man, not just one or the other."[31] Historian and Editor Steven Waldman writes, "Most of the Founding Fathers at one point believed in a God who intervened in the lives of Americans."[32] Imagine if the Founding Fathers operated under another worldview. What would the United States be like?

The biblical worldview can be seen in the leadership of many companies as well. Companies like Chick-Fil-A, ServiceMaster, Hobby Lobby, and Covenant Transportation all run on Judeo-Christian values and were founded on the biblical worldview.[33] Other worldviews including Atheism, Buddhism, Hinduism, and Islam have had significant impact on corporations around the world. Worldviews do have an impact on the marketplace. Why is this so important?

Decisions, policies, processes and people in the workplace all have been influenced, either directly or indirectly, by worldviews. Every employee, manager or executive has his or her own worldview. We must understand this in order to recognize why it has become more increasingly difficult to integrate Christianity at work. There is constant friction in the spiritual world. We are communicated to through television, music, social media sites, periodicals, etc. that all have been influenced by worldviews. We are told that religion is private. Religion should not be part of the workplace. We see television series where Christianity is portrayed in a negative light or is directly assaulted. This is all through influence of worldviews. In their book *How Now Shall We Live?,* authors Chuck Colson and Nancy Pearson state, "a debilitating weakness in modern evangelicalism is that we've been fighting cultural skirmishes on all sides without knowing what the war itself is about. We have not identified the worldviews that lie at the root of cultural conflict—and this ignorance dooms our best efforts...The real war is a cosmic struggle between worldviews—between the Christian worldview and the various other secular and spiritual worldviews arrayed against it. This is what we must understand if we are going to be effective in evangelizing our world today and in transforming it to reflect the wisdom of the Creator."[34] In order for the Christian to be effective in the workplace, he or she must understand the forces at work. This is why the spiritual disciplines and the practice thereof are so important—more in a later chapter.

The biblical worldview of work is simple. God created man to work. He gave us dominion over creation and commanded Adam to take care of the land. Work was part of worship to God. Work was a joyful activity. The fall into sin changed the parameters and consequences came as a result, but that does not change God's intention for work. For the Christian, our worldview is that God does exist and he is actively engaged in the affairs of men including providing salvation (from eternal separation) to all who believe and accept him. Our worldview also holds that there is both good (God) and evil (Satan or the Devil) and that human nature is born into sin through a series of events at the time of creation (the story of Adam and Eve in the book of Genesis). Our worldview also holds that God is omniscient (all-knowing), omnipresent (everywhere present) and omnipotent (all-powerful). These tenets of our worldview are very important as they lay the foundation for how we should view and live our lives. For example, if we truly believe that God is omnipresent then we can assume he is with us on the job. If he is with us on the job, then he sees our performance on the job including our behavior and decisions.

For employers and companies, this has huge implications. Employees with this worldview (and who truly follow it) will work with integrity and high ethics because that is what God desires and if he is present everywhere, he sees and knows their actions. Of course this is not to say that all Christians make better employees. All too often I have managed employees who were Christians and were some of my worst performers. I am simply suggesting that worldviews do have an impact on the workplace, directly or indirectly. Nancy Pearcey tells the story of a Congress member who once told her, "I got involved in politics after the 1973 abortion decision because I thought that was the fastest route to moral reform. Well, we've won some legislative victories, but we've lost the culture." She went on to say that the most effective work, he had come to realize, is done by ordinary Christians fulfilling God's calling to reform culture within their local spheres of influence—their families, churches, schools, neighborhoods, workplaces, professional organizations, and civic institutions. In order to effect lasting change, the congressman concluded, "We need to develop a

Christian worldview."[35] I could not agree more. How you view life will impact how you work. It's that simple. Christians can be effective in the workplace following the biblical worldview. Our performance should reflect what Christ expects of us. Was Jesus a poor performing carpenter? I don't think so by any means. Was the apostle Paul an average tentmaker? I don't think so. I believe Jesus and Paul knew the value of their examples at work and ensured they worked as unto the Lord.

While this is not an exhaustive study on worldviews nor was it intended to be, it is important to understand your worldview and its relationship to your work performance.

In Summary:

Do you have a biblical worldview? Why or why not?

_____

_____

_____

_____

_____

_____

Why is our worldview so important to our jobs? Do you believe this? Why or why not?

_____

_____

_____

_____

_____

_____

_____

Have you seen or heard examples of other worldviews in the workplace? What were they?

_____

_____

_____

_____

_____

_____

Do you agree with the biblical worldview of work? Why or why not?

_____

_____

_____

_____

_____

_____

Sample prayer for understanding a biblical worldview:

> *Lord Jesus,*
>
> *Help me to understand the biblical worldview and apply it to my life. Open my heart, mind, and soul to your word, commands, and love. Transform my mind into the person you want me to be. Give me experiences and opportunities to better learn your worldview that I may teach it to others, whether by living example or witnessing or perhaps both.*
>
> *Amen.*

Chapter 2

Better Performance at Work
with Spiritual Disciplines

The most effective way to improve your workplace performance and your leadership skills is to incorporate spiritual disciplines into your life consistently. You may be asking "what do spiritual disciplines have to do with the integration of faith, work and better performance on the job?" The answer is simple. Everything.

Let's quickly define the difference between discipline and habit. Discipline is not habit. There is a difference. Habits do not necessarily improve skills or character. At some point, a habit does not require active thought. Discipline on the other hand should always require proactive thought. The definition of discipline is an activity, exercise, or a regimen that develops or improves a skill. The definition of habit is an acquired behavior pattern regularly followed until it has become almost involuntary.

Spiritual disciplines include many areas such as study of the Bible, prayer, fasting, worship, serving, and solitude. Disciplines such as these enable us to break down the chains of sin, frustration, incompetence, greed and selfishness. From a Christian's perspective, God is "all-sufficient" meaning that He has guidance for every area of life. Since this is the hypothesis, one can test it by spending more time in the disciplines. God states that we are to cast our cares upon him, for he cares for us.[36] These cares include the workplace and our careers. His

Word also states that we are to seek him first above everything else. Matthew, the tax collector turned Apostle, listening to Christ preach the sermon on the mount, penned the following, "Seek ye first the Kingdom of God and his righteousness; and all these things shall be added unto you."[37] What "added things" was he referring to? Earlier in the sermon Christ spoke of food, clothing and other things that fill our minds. Simply put, Jesus was stating to focus on the things of God first and everything else will fall into place. Now this does not mean we "ignore" the workplace or segregate it. On the contrary, it means to put God first in the workplace and in your jobs. Seek out his will and wisdom for your career and performance objectives.

I have seen the results from practicing spiritual disciplines in the lives of my family and in my own life as well. By spending daily time in God's word and in prayer, I have felt strengthened, encouraged, creative, humbled, and joy-filled. Lack of time in the disciplines has made me less alert, frustrated at times, and with a lack of fulfillment in life in general. Though by no means is this example statistically valid, I challenge you to try it for yourselves. My grandfather, Joseph Taylor, was a painter by trade. In fact, he was well known for the excellence he brought to every paint job he was a part of. He was also a preacher who was the Senior Pastor of Wayside Chapel, a small church of 150 people give or take. For eleven years, my grandfather worked both trades, painter and preacher, giving his best at both. He knew how to integrate his faith with his work, and men on the job with him knew he was a Christian. My grandfather also spent time on his knees and in the Word of God every day. He, along with my grandmother, would spend hours in prayer (a lost activity in today's modern fast paced world). As I was growing up, I witnessed their daily examples and how they influenced my parents, aunts and uncles. As a family, we practiced spiritual disciplines together no matter where we were. We gave thanks at every meal whether at Denny's, Spires, or Don Jose's. We prayed and read the Bible while on vacation or during weekend trips to the high desert where the family owns property. I heard stories from many of the family members how they happened to share their faith at work or how a co-worker had accepted Christ. In parallel, we were always expected to perform our best at any job "because we work as unto the Lord", a favorite saying of my parents and others. I realize not everyone had the blessing of growing up with that type of family heritage, but we all can start somewhere.

It all starts with the basics. As Christians we need to continue to learn about our faith and more important, God's Word, and this in turn will help with our behaviors, both on and off the job. Dallas Willard in his latest book states, "Not having knowledge of the central truths of Christianity is certainly one reason for the great disparity between what Christians profess and how they behave—a well-known and disturbing phenomenon."[38] It is our continual efforts in exercising the spiritual disciplines that will truly change who we are, both internally and externally. These disciplines must be exercised during our normal day-to-day lives. We must not wait until some special moment or service or when the time is right. Richard Foster states, "The discovery of God lies in the daily and the ordinary, not in the spectacular and the heroic. If we cannot find God in the routines of home and shop, then we will not find him at all."[39] I truly believe this statement. God is the God of every day, not just Sundays or your specific day of worship.

So what are these disciplines? The rest of this chapter will briefly discuss each discipline. There are more scholarly works on this subject and I highly recommend books by authors such as Richard Foster and Dallas Willard for a deeper understanding of the transformative nature of the spiritual disciplines.

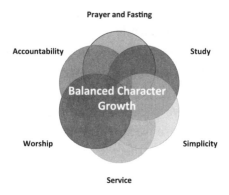

Prayer and Fasting

Prayer changes things. My father prayed for his fellow firefighters regularly. On at least five occasions, he was able to lead someone to the Lord at work through the power of prayer. Two of his friends that he led to the Lord went on to become involved in ministries of their own including worship leading and a Messianic Jewish ministry in Israel. It all started through prayer. We have all heard stories of answered prayer and we have all understood what it is like to pray and seemingly receive "no answer." But God always answers prayer. It may not be in our time, or the way we want the answer to turn out to be, but he always answers prayer. My family prayed for my grandfather to be healed of bone cancer for two years. Here was a man of God who had served the Lord with fervency both in the workplace and as a full-time pastor reduced to mere pounds and in agonizing pain. God finally answered our prayers by taking my grandpa home. I may not understand God's timing in answering those prayers but I do understand he knows all things and works all things for good to those that are called.

The Bible commands us to pray always and it was so important that Jesus gave us a model of prayer.[40] We know it as the Lord's Prayer. *Our Father which art in heaven, hallowed be thy name. Thy Kingdom come, thy will be done on earth as it is in Heaven. Give us this day our daily bread and forgive us our debts and we forgive our debtors. And lead us not into temptation but deliver us from evil for thine is the kingdom and the power and the glory forever. Amen.* In this model we see a very clear pattern for prayer. This does not mean we need to fall into legalism when praying (legalists would say you must say exactly these words in this order or you blaspheme). While there are much better theological explanations of the Lord's Prayer, I have described the pattern in my own words. The pattern is reverential worship, requesting God's will (perhaps in others' lives, in our own lives, etc.), prayer for needs (again this applies to praying for others' needs as well), forgiveness of sins and the help to forgive others who have hurt us, deliverance and general worship. All that we ever need to pray for fits into this pattern. But let's not get hung up on the pattern. God hears a three word prayer as well. The key is to pray with an open heart and willing mind.

Yet, why is prayer so difficult sometimes? Disbelief, lack of faith, emotions gone awry, busyness, laziness or lack of discipline are just some of the reasons people do not pray. The apostle Paul tells us that we are to pray without ceasing.[41] This simply means to be in an attitude of prayer at all times. Communication with God can happen anytime, day or night. I often pray before going into an important meeting. I ask the Lord for wisdom and strength to give my best in the meeting. He has answered so many times, even when I was physically sick and traveling. The book of James tells us that fervent prayer gets results.[42] Sometimes we need to be in focused prayer. Most important, Jesus himself prayed. If Christ felt it important enough to pray, then we have no excuse in not praying. One of the most beautiful prayers recorded in the Bible is prayed by Jesus.[43]

Take time to pray. Spend quality time on your knees before God. Get away to a quiet place, perhaps a conference room, a backyard, or a bathroom. Wherever you can find a place, pray.

I often pray as I drive. Instead of listening to news, business shows, sports shows or music, sometimes I pray. Fasting is a deeper, higher form of prayer and God takes it very seriously.[44] Fasting is where you give up something to symbolically sacrifice for something you need God to answer. Food is the typical sacrifice. Fasting, when done right and in proper context, can be a very powerful discipline. There are many great books on fasting and I recommend you learn more before you fast.

More than leather, pages and ink (Study)

One of my most prized possessions is an old study Bible used by my grandfather in ministry. It is fifty-two years old at the time of this writing and given to him by my grandmother at Christmas in 1958. She wrote an inscription on the inside cover page that is powerful and has been shared through generations of our family. I am not sure if the writing came from another author or if my grandmother penned it herself. In either case, as you read it, let it speak to you. The inscription reads as follows: *This Book contains the mind of God, the state of man, way of salvation, doom of sinners and happiness of believers. Its doctrines are holy, its precepts are binding, its histories are true, and its decisions are immutable. Read it to be wise, believe it to be safe, and practice it to be holy. It contains light to direct you, food to support you, and comfort to cheer you. It is the travelers map, the pilgrims staff, the pilots compass, the soldiers sword, and the Christians charter. Christ is its grand subject, our good its design and the gory of God its end. It should fill the memory, rule the head, and guide the feet. Read it slowly, prayerfully. It is a mine of wealth, a paradise of glory, and a river of pleasure. It is given you in life, will be opened at the judgment, and be remembered forever. It involves the highest responsibility, rewards the greatest labor, and condemns all who trifle with its holy contents.* My grandparents understood the power of God's word and taught each of their children to absorb themselves in its pages. As a grandchild, it is the thing I am most grateful for.

The most powerful book ever written is indeed a collection of sixty-six books. Have you ever wondered how this could be? Or what the odds are that such a book would last for thousands of years (written over a span of 5,500 plus years)? This alone has to make you think about its authenticity. Why has this book, the Holy Bible, been so revered yet at the same time, so criticized? There has to be something to this collection of books and letters.

Let me start by stating that my objective here is not to argue for or debate the authenticity of the Bible as I am assuming the reader has already agreed to its value and purpose. My objective here is to encourage the reader to establish and maintain the discipline of consistently reading and studying the Word of God. Of course, this is nothing new. Leaders, parents, business people, politicians, soldiers, tradesmen and philosophers throughout history have spoken about the value of studying and spending time in reading the Bible. Abraham Lincoln once said, "I am profitably engaged in reading the Bible. Take all of this Book that you can by reason and the balance by faith, and you will live and die a better man." A.W. Tozer (twentieth century preacher and theologian) wrote, "The Word of God well understood and religiously obeyed is the shortest route to spiritual perfection. And we must not select a few favorite passages to the exclusion of others. Nothing less than the whole Bible can make a whole Christian."[45]

At this time, I would encourage you to grab your Bible and as you review the rest of this section, read each Scripture reference and let God speak to your heart.

As a Christian, we are commanded to study the Word. Both the Old Testament and New Testament contain Scriptures that tell us to read God's Word and also of the value in doing so. The prophet Isaiah wrote "Seek ye out the book of the Lord and read…"[46] Jesus Christ himself told us (as written in the book of John) to search the Scriptures.[47] The value in doing so is extraordinary. The list of benefits one receives in reading the Bible is astounding. Review the following carefully and reflect on the impact these benefits would have in your life including the workplace. Reading and studying God's Word minimizes sin in our lives, cleanses our hearts, gives us liberty, provides comfort, builds knowledge and wisdom, guides our steps, grows understanding, fosters hope, fills with joy, sets foundation of truth, and enables peace in our lives.[48] Now, let's apply some of this to the marketplace and to our current job. Every one of these benefits has a direct relationship to your performance on the job. Think about it carefully. If you were filled with eternal hope and joy, the "little" problems at work would pale in comparison (not that they are not real and sometimes important). When God says he will guide our steps and give us wisdom and knowledge, he did not say "except in your professional lives." The world may have segregated our private and professional lives but God did not. He gives us wisdom and guidance for all areas of life including how to be a better interior designer, scientist, accountant, chief operations officer, teacher, firefighter, etc. If God is all knowing (omniscient), wouldn't he know all about atoms, mathematics, language, marketing, relationships, leadership, strategy, risk management, etc.? By reading the Bible and asking God to help us apply it to our lives (including our jobs), then he will do so and more.

An example of this in my own life is what I call the E9:10 Principle (nothing fancy with the name, just a help in memory for Eccles. 9:10). In Ecclesiastes 9:10, King Solomon (who according to the Bible was the wisest man to have ever lived) wrote, "whatsoever thy hand findeth to do, *do it with thy might…*" (emphasis added). The second half of the verse gives the reason why. We only have one life to achieve everything we want to achieve according to His purpose. The apostle Matthew (a Tax Collector by trade) writes, "lay not up for yourselves treasures upon earth where moth and rust doth corrupt… but lay up for yourselves treasures in heaven…"[49]

By combining these two commands, I have strived to be a top performer in my job and in everything I do while also balancing my life by serving others for the sake of God's kingdom. There are two key reasons why we are to give our best in everything we do. The apostle Paul (a Tentmaker by trade) gives us the primary reason when he writes that "…whatsoever we do, do it heartily, as to the Lord, and not unto men; knowing that of the Lord ye shall receive the reward of the inheritance: for ye serve the Lord Christ."[50] First and foremost, we are to work as unto Christ and not to our manager. In doing so, Christ will honor our work and provide opportunity for growth. The second key reason for giving your best is that your performance will provide a platform for opportunities to tell others about what God has done for you. As noted in the opening story, Francis Schaeffer, a noted Christian Philosopher, stated, "If you do your work well, you will have a chance to speak."[51] Your fellow co-workers, customers, suppliers, and your management will all wonder how you do it. You will be asked questions like "how have you maintained such high performance?" or "how did you balance your objectives while achieving results?" Questions like these, especially in an informal setting like a business lunch or dinner, may provide an opportunity for you to discuss your trust in God and his support. If you are an average or mediocre performer, then even if you confidently witness in the workplace, people will question your talk with your walk. As a side note, always doing your job well, gives you a chance to be a voice of change, improvement or innovation as well. Leadership, customers and peers alike will listen more to a high-performer than to someone who is average or mediocre in performance.

So how do we make the most of studying God's word? Richard Foster (Pastor and Theologian) writes that there are four steps to studying: Repetition, Concentration, Comprehension and Reflection.[52] Take a moment and think about these four steps. Reading the Bible should be done following these four steps. One should study the Bible with repetition enabling penetration within the mind building memory. In doing so, a Christian can recall Scripture when facing trials, a crisis, through celebration, etc. Concentrating on Scripture enables the Christian to focus on the pages of wisdom without being distracted by the cares of life, including the workplace. Comprehension is completed when the first two steps are done and a Christian comprehends the meaning of what he or she is reading. Reflection enables the reader to understand the Scripture's impact personally and its application to daily life. If you focus on these steps as you develop your study discipline, you will quickly improve your knowledge of the Bible leading to a stronger relationship with Christ.

Keep it simple

Simplicity these days is all but vanished. I am not speaking about the ways we conduct business or how we perform activities throughout our daily lives. Everyone would agree the continued innovation of technology has simplified life in numerous ways. For example, we can now search for directions on the web to anywhere in the world reducing time and stress. We fly from Los Angeles to London non-stop in under ten hours easing the way we do global business. We have software and applications that automate processes increasing productivity and quality exponentially in many industries. We can receive text messages or mobile calls asking us to pick up one more item at the store eliminating the need to go back to the store a second time.

While these and other innovations have made life simpler, when I speak of simplicity I mean as an outlook on life in general. All too often we clutter our minds and lives with activities, fears, doubts, mistakes, greed, etc. that drain the energy levels of the mind and spirit. We justify these sometimes by saying we are pursuing career goals, wanting to retire early or other excuses when in reality they do not help us to perform better. There is nothing wrong with goals, objectives and hard work to achieve them. But if we do not prioritize our lives with what's deeply important (some may not even understand their purpose in life) versus what can be done away with, we will miss the true mark that God has in store for His people in all areas of life.

Paul, a tentmaker and writer of letters in the Bible, wrote of contentment to the church at Philippi. He captures the essence of simplicity with these words "…for I have learned, in whatsoever state I am, therewith to be content."[53] This has enormous value for our jobs as well. Imagine if we all prayed for contentment in what God has given us in the workplace. What would your day be like at work if you were filled with internal contentment in Christ even when faced with problems, challenges, and risks? Look at the book of Hebrews for a moment. We are told to stop coveting (including traits such as envy, jealousy and greed) and be content with what we have. Why? The verse goes on to say that Christ said I will never leave you or forsake you.[54]

So if we took this to work with us, we would look at our jobs differently recognizing that Christ is ever-present with us. Does this mean we should not want career growth? Does it mean that we should have the attitude that where we are, is where we will remain because, after all, be content? This is a falsehood. As we have already seen, we are to give our very best in our jobs as unto the Lord. I guarantee you that if you live and work by this principle, you will reap the rewards of promotional growth. It will become a natural byproduct of your giving honor to God in everything you do. However, as you do your best, remember to ask God for contentment in His wisdom for your life.

Serving Others (A servant's heart)

"You want to transform the workplace, take on an attitude of servanthood."[55] I was sitting in the service at Hillsong London

Church when the Senior Pastor made this statement during his sermon. It is a simple statement but so very true. Much has been written about servanthood in business leadership books. While many of the books are very good, I would refer you to the Bible itself. Clearly, there are many Scriptures that speak directly about serving others and some command us to do it. In the Gospel of John, the Apostle tells us a story about how Jesus washed the feet of the disciples.[56] Reflect on the scene for a moment. After dinner, Jesus got up and began to prepare the necessary items for washing feet. He humbled himself even in his dress as he removed his outer clothing so I am sure as not to get them wet or dirty. He wrapped himself in the towel that he would later dry each of the disciples' feet with. I am very sure (as Peter even gives us an example) the disciples were very unsure of what was taking place and some afraid or concerned. They all believed (except for Judas) this was truly the Son of God and here He was bending down and washing and drying their feet (culturally, people washed their feet as they entered homes due to the dust and dirt from walking about). After finishing the task, Jesus then closes with the statement, "If I then, your Lord and Master, have washed your feet; ye also ought to wash one another's feet. For I have given you an example, that ye should do as I have done to you."[57]

How can we apply this to our workplace? Have you ever thought about how you can "wash the feet" of your fellow peers, employees you manage, customers you service or managers you report to? As a manager, I can think of several ways I have tried to do this. One way is to get to know your employee/s personally. Understand who they are and how they think. Although this takes time, it will be well worth the investment because once you understand a little of where they are coming from, you can invest in actions that will serve them such as helping them to achieve development goals even if it means for future work outside of your division or your company. I have had several employees who had interests in other career paths outside of the company that I have given support to. There are many ways to balance value to the current company and the employee's future goals. Developing excellence with the customer experience crosses all industries and careers for example.

Serving is not always easy but will lead to dynamic relationships and excellent results. This also means serving the company you work for. Again, we work as unto the Lord and in doing so, that means we work for Christ no matter what company we are employed with. We may not always agree with the policies and procedures of our employers but we need to recognize what true servanthood is. It's about sacrifice of our own wants to ensure others' needs are met.

Worshipping God increases productivity

When we worship our Creator and Savior, he draws near to our praises. The Bible says the Lord takes pleasure in His people.[58] He takes pleasure in those that fear Him and hope in His mercy.[59] We are told that everything that has breath should praise the Lord.[60] There are many examples throughout Scripture of God's people worshipping him in many different ways. Elijah, Moses, Hannah, Ruth, David, Daniel, Noah, and Abraham are just some of those examples. The apostle Paul wrote to the church at Ephesus to sing hymns and songs, making melody in your hearts to God and giving thanks for all God and Christ have done.[61]

You may be asking yourself, "so what does this have to do with my workplace or job performance?" There are two good reasons that I will share. The first is that we should want to worship Christ and all he has done. By studying His word and praying more, you will naturally find yourself worshipping Him more even at work. The second is that if we are obedient to God's Word in all things including worship, then God will honor our lives with His wisdom and blessing, yes even at work. Worship brings our focus and attention on Christ. It allows us to stand still in His presence (whether it's viewing nature, activities with family, etc.) and realize our purpose in life is to worship him through all of our activities. He takes pleasure in that as we have seen. Question for reflection: does he take pleasure in your worship?

This intense focus on Him through worship allows us to rejuvenate for actions or things that we have to accomplish. Many times during my business travels I have seen a beautiful bird or meadow and thought "Lord, thank you for your creation." I have spent many hours and miles 35,000 plus feet in the air and have witnessed awesome storms, lightning shows, sunrises, sunsets and full moons. His wonders never cease to amaze me. In reality, these small forms of worship sometimes between e-mails on my laptop have helped me stay focused and energized. I have a sense of purpose greater than my job which in turn enables better performance on the job.

Accountability

Do you have anyone in your life that is holding you accountable to your Christian walk, your job performance and/ or your personal goals and objectives? If not, why not? Proverbs states that he who walks with wise men shall be wise but a companion of fools shall be destroyed.[62] It also states that open rebuke is better than secret love and faithful are the wounds of a friend.[63] Accountability is holding oneself to be accountable for all your actions. But one cannot be accountable alone. First, we must be accountable to God through the lens of his word. Second, we must find a core group of friends, mentors or both that we can trust with our accountability. This is what accountability is all about. Having a group of wise friends who will listen to your mistakes, goals, decisions and concerns and help you grow with and from them. We were not created to "go it alone." We were created to hear the wise counsel of others, to hear the rebuke from others as iron sharpens iron as yet another proverb states. We are to sharpen each other to make us stronger, better.[64]

If you are not in a small group or accountability team, I would urge you to start one or join one. It only has to be two people although it's best if it is three to four in my experience. This is nothing new in the workplace. Mentoring is highly regarded, and part of mentoring is learning from your mistakes and being accountable to them. We will discuss accountability more in the Leadership chapter of this book.

In Summary:

Which spiritual discipline appeals to you? Or seems to be a natural fit?

_____

_____

_____

_____

_____

Which spiritual discipline is most difficult for you? Why?

_____

_____

_____

_____

_____

Why do you think reading God's Word is so difficult at times?

_____

_____

_____

_____

_____

Simplicity is not always easy to do in today's modern world. Why?

_____

_____

_____

_____

_____

When was the last time God answered a prayer you had?

_____

_____

_____

_____

_____

Sample prayer for spiritual disciplines:

> *Lord Jesus,*
>
> *Open my heart to your disciplines. Give me strength, fortitude, perseverance and will to practice these disciplines in my life. Place a burning desire in my heart to be holy before you. Draw me to your word daily. Teach me to pray often, to listen to your voice, and to reflect on your creation. Transform my life daily.*
>
> *Amen.*

Chapter 3

Grab your Bibles, Leaders!

Biblical Leadership enhances Marketplace Success

Thousands of books have been written on leadership throughout history, many of them very good and many of them not so good. One can walk into a local mainstream bookstore and find literally over a hundred titles on leadership from all walks of life. Even with all of these resources and research, the study of leadership will continue to grow and develop. The primary reason is the crucial impact leadership (whether good or bad) has on life. Leadership and its various forms thread through the fabric of life, from parenting to business to relationships to religion. Everyone in some way has had an opportunity to lead in some capacity such as in friendship, in parenthood, playing sports, or in the workplace. Every one is a leader in some way.

The English Preacher and Theologian John Stott once stated, "Christian leadership ...appears to break down into five main ingredients—clear vision, hard work, dogged perseverance, humble service, and iron discipline." When you consider these "ingredients," you can certainly see the relationship to the business world as well. These ingredients are much needed in today's leaders. Imagine if the leaders of today had clear vision, worked hard, had strong perseverance, were humble and had iron discipline. Our commerce and marketplaces would never be the same. Before we dig deeper into the area of leadership, let's quickly define leadership. Webster's 1828

Edition Dictionary defines a leader as: "One that leads or conducts; a guide; a conductor; a commander; a captain." The next definition states, "One who goes first." The definition of leading states, "showing the way by going first." The modern definition of leadership (Webster's On-Line) is: "The office or position of a leader; capacity to lead; the act or instance of leading." Leadership is about going first. First in developing then sharing the vision, motivating the team, getting results, serving others and showing discipline. Eagle Peak Leadership simply defines leadership as "the ability to influence through several means which enables the achievement of results." The "means" could be authority, experience, knowledge, or a combination of all three.

How do you view leadership? Do you "show the way by going first?" Do you have a capacity to lead, and if so, how are you developing that capacity? Leadership skills: Are you born with them or do you learn them? Leadership can be developed in everyone even when you are not "born with leadership abilities." Successful leaders never stop learning—even when the results are exponentially positive. True Leadership then develops leaders who in turn develop more leaders. Authentic leaders generate organizational excitement about continuous development.

That is the purpose of this chapter. I want to generate excitement in you about the biblical impact on leadership and how principles from the Bible can accelerate your leadership performance while deepening your relationships with shareholders, employees, peers, customers and suppliers. Leadership is nothing new. There may be different styles of leadership or approaches taken, but clearly it is nothing new. In fact, many of today's leadership styles and approaches come straight from the Bible and biblical values. Richard Donkin, a leader on employment in the U.K., writes of the Bible's influence on leadership during an example given regarding the leadership styles Jim Collins uses in his book *Good to Great*. Donkin writes of the leadership style using steely resolve, purpose, tempered by fairness and compassion, "…Except that the style is not new (steely resolve, purpose, tempered by fairness and compassion)." It was as old as the Bible since these sympathies are reflected in Christian values. We can see this ancient heritage in most forms of leadership. Leadership, like work, is as old as the soil."[65] J. Oswald Sanders in his great book on leadership[66] developed a table that showed some of the differences between the secular worldview of leadership and biblical worldview of leadership. The table looks like this:

Secular Worldview of Leadership	Biblical Worldview of Leadership
Self-confident	Confident in God
Knows men	Also knows God
Makes own decisions	Seeks God's Will
Ambitious	Humble
Creates methods	Follows God's example
Enjoys command	Delights in obedience to God
Seeks personal reward	Loves God and others
Independent	Depends on God

Notice the emphasis on God in the biblical worldview. This does not mean that all the elements under the secular worldview are necessarily bad. In fact, all are good when managed with balance and control. The intent is to get you thinking about the differences. That's all. So how do we develop a better worldview of leadership? What characteristics does the Bible call out that we can apply to leadership? There are many characteristics that a leader should develop in his or her life; however, I believe there are six core characteristics that should be developed first, all biblically based. These six characteristics interact with each other and any weakness in one will drive weakness in others automatically.

The six characteristics are having a spirit-filled vision, integrity, developing spiritual disciplines, serving others, communication, and having a sense of urgency. Of course, there are other characteristics (represented by one of the circles) that we do not want to forget about like time management, risk taking, strategic thinking, etc. Again, these should be developed as well, but if a leader starts with the six characteristics first, they will find it easier to develop the others. For example, if the leader has a very clear vision, then developing strategy, taking risks or driving results can be easier to lead. Vision drives strategy, vision can motivate risk taking, and vision can drive results as passion for the vision builds.

Let's briefly review the six characteristics and what the Bible says about them. As we look at spirit- filled vision, let's break up the phrase and look at what it means to be spirit-filled first. The Bible states that as Christians the Spirit of God resides within us as a guide and encourager, but also provides direction and conviction when we make wrong decisions or choices (such as sin).[67] As we walk through our lives with

Him as our guide we should see the "fruit" of walking in the Spirit.[68] Paul the tentmaker wrote to the church in Galatia and through the inspiration of God gave them what the fruit of the Spirit should be. This fruit includes love, joy, peace, patience, kindness, goodness, faithfulness, gentleness and self-control. By accepting Christ as King of our life (enabling his Spirit to dwell within us) and living according to His commandments (The Bible), we will yield this fruit in our lives.[69]

Carefully consider the application of this truth to the marketplace or more specifically your company and/or job. How much better of an employee, team member, peer, customer, supplier, etc. would you be if you truly were filled with the fruit of the Spirit? When the deadlines loom, the peace of God can sustain you. When others frustrate or impede the progress of your work, the kindness and goodness of God will ensure you are balanced and fair when dealing with the issue (note this does not mean you ignore the issue). When revenues and profits slip and the market is screaming for results, the patience of God will strengthen you. We all can think of numerous examples of how the fruit of the Spirit can help us at work. Another important critical benefit of being filled with the fruit of the Spirit is that this fruit will better prepare businesses and individuals to set good vision.

The second part of the phrase "spirit-filled vision" is the word vision itself. Setting good vision is critical to anyone's success in life and applies to business, marriage, parenting, friendships, etc. Some areas of life will not be as formal in vision setting but nonetheless there will be vision. For example, as a parent, my wife and I had a set vision of "loving and developing our children to be lovers of God, morally grounded, hard working and positive contributors in society."

Most good businesses as well as individuals who want to excel set good visions. The Bible states, "Where there is no vision, the people perish..."[70] Vision gives purpose. Vision provides the ultimate goal. Vision enables people. Closely tied to vision is purpose. As stated, vision gives the purpose for an organization. It answers the question what is the purpose of the organization? What is the purpose of my division, my department, my job? Purpose and meaning are very important to human nature. David and Wendy Ulrich, in their compelling book *The Why of Work*, write, "Obviously, people find meaning in many settings—in the privacy of homes and the expanses of nature, in churches, ballparks, and community centers, in family and friendship circles. But work takes the lion's share of our time and energy. Most of us spend more time at work than at play, at family gatherings, at religious meetings, or at hobbies. The organizations in which we labor are thus a primary setting not only for accomplishing assignments but also for finding an abiding sense of meaning in life. Work is a universal setting in which to pursue our universal search for meaning."[71] Meaning at work inter-relates to finding purpose at work. We all long for purpose. One the best books written on leadership in several years came out this year authored by Joel Kurtzman. Kurtzman's overall thesis is that through the power of common purpose, leaders can get organizations to achieve the extraordinary. Purpose has been lost in many of today's workplaces. Kurtzman gives good examples of organizations who have achieved common purpose leadership.[72] The bottom line is that vision and purpose bring real value to the workplace and to the overall marketplace as well.

The second biblical characteristic of leadership is Integrity. Integrity is proven to impact economics and has direct correlation to financial performance. According to author Anna Bernasek,

"Integrity is so critical to our economic performance that it can explain disparities in national wealth."[73] Bernasek gives many economic examples and explores financial data through hypothesis testing including regression analysis to prove integrity impacts economics. For example, there are twelve relationships of trust in an average ATM transaction including relationships between the Bank, the National Network, the ATM company, the Clearing House, and of course the person performing the ATM transaction.[74] Much has been written on integrity; however, having "real" integrity is only possible through a relationship with God. Why? Because God is the only one who can change the internal nature of man. Without God, all people are sinners and prone to evil thoughts and actions. By having integrity founded in Christ, we can achieve so much more in our relationships whether at home, work or in our communities. What does integrity give you?

According to the Bible, integrity preserves your life, protects against judgment, must be a conscious decision to walk therein, provides guidance, and passes blessings to posterity (children).[75] With those benefits, who would not want to have the integrity founded on God's Word? The life of Joseph as read in the book of Genesis has long been used as a primary example of someone who had real integrity when faced with temptations. But there are many others as well. Job showed integrity even when he lost everything. Daniel showed integrity to the point where his enemies had been looking for a falsehood or sin and could not find one. In fact, they had to build their case on his integrity. They knew he would not bow down to anyone except God. They counted on Daniel to keep his integrity so that he would be considered guilty. Little did they realize that Daniel's integrity was founded on God's love for him and the enemies paid for it with their own lives and that of their families.[76]

The example of Micaiah is one of my favorites in Scripture regarding integrity. The Israeli King Ahab had asked the King of Judah, Jehoshaphat, to align with him in war against a common enemy. Jehoshaphat asks Ahab to inquire of the Lord through the prophets. It is stated that 400 prophets all agreed that both Kings should engage in the battle because victory is guaranteed. Jehoshaphat does not quite believe in these prophets and asks if there is another. Ahab reluctantly tells him of another prophet named Micaiah who has historically prophesied negatively towards King Ahab. They send for Micaiah and as Micaiah is being brought to the kings, he is told about how these 400 prophets had already prophesied positive results and that he should do the same. Micaiah replies, "As the Lord lives, what my God says, that will I speak."[77] Micaiah must have felt enormous pressure but it did not show. He knew where his integrity belonged. Micaiah ends up prophesying the death of Ahab and the loss of battle. He is imprisoned for doing so and mocked by the other prophets. Both kings proceed into battle and Ahab is struck down and killed and the battle is indeed lost.

There are many important lessons regarding integrity in this story. First, no matter how many others stand against what you believe in, do not give in or give up. The second principle is that sometimes standing on our integrity will cause significant sacrifice, pain or frustration. Rest in knowing that integrity founded on Christ will stand eternally. The third principle is that many times we surround ourselves with people who tell us what we want to hear and not what we should be hearing. Do you allow your peers, employees, or mentors to give you constructive criticism? Do you give constructive criticism even though it may not be popular to do so? The fourth and final principle is sometimes it is not good to jump into something without trusted data, counsel and other information. Integrity enables a leader to follow the right path after careful consideration. Jehoshaphat barely escaped with his life, but only because he had enough integrity to cry out to God for help.

Earlier in this book, I devoted a chapter to the importance of spiritual disciplines so I won't spend time on this characteristic in this chapter, however, it is vital to leadership development. The next biblical characteristic of Leadership is serving others. The idea of serving others at work seems odd when you deal with it strictly from a secular viewpoint. All too often people associate serving with weakness. If you serve another team member such as preparing more than your share of a required report, it is sometimes viewed as showing weakness. This is especially true when dealing with suppliers or other departments within your own organization. Many corporations view their suppliers as subordinates and the idea of serving your supplier is perceived as a negative business practice.

The Gospel of Mark[78] (The Gospel of Matthew shares this story as well.) shares a story of how Christ set the expectation of serving others with his twelve Apostles. It all started with two of the disciples asking Jesus for placement at his right and left hand when Christ came fully into his kingdom (All of the Apostles firmly believed that Christ was the Messiah and was there to set up the Kingdom.). This bold request was rejected by Christ and when the ten other Apostles heard it, they became angry (the King James Version states "much displeased"). Let's stop here to compare these types of emotions to our workplaces and jobs. Have you ever had a peer or have known of someone who promoted themselves to the boss or manager or asked for a favor applying to them only? Perhaps they did this at the expense of others? We all have been through something like this. The brothers James and John probably did not intend to offend the others with their request, yet their request certainly implied they deserved promotion above the others. What was Christ's response? It is interesting to note that Christ addressed all twelve with his response as he saw the same character flaw in each one of them.

Jesus calmly replied that while the standard for leadership of the day was leadership of strict authority, he wanted the Apostles to have no part in that (this does not mean that Christ dismisses the authority of leadership). Jesus stated that whoever was to be "great" among them must also be the servant. He went on to state that even the "first" must be the "slave of all." The example he gave was the leadership he exhibited himself. He stated that he did not come to Earth to be ministered to but to minister to others. Reflect on this a moment. This is real difficult to live out in the workplace at times, isn't it? Leaders expect to give direction, provide vision, remove barriers, and make bold decisions. It is not necessarily an expectation to "serve" others. According to Jesus, it should be.

Good communication is the next biblical characteristic of leadership we find critical to work success (and for life in general of course). The Bible gives us a simple but very effective model for communication.[79] James the Apostle writes, "Wherefore, my beloved brethren, let every man be swift to hear, slow to speak, slow to wrath." A simple, but profound Scripture and truth. Let's break it down. James first states, "let every man be swift to hear." Active listening is critical. Train yourself to listen to someone carefully and ask for clarification if you do not understand their communication. We should want to listen more than we want to speak. Why? By listening intently and carefully, we can avoid miscommunication, we can build better relationships, and we can increase knowledge faster.

The second statement in the verse is that every man should be "slow to speak." We are to think before we speak. Too often people "blurt" out statements that they later regret or others regret hearing. Have you ever done so? I am reminded of a customer meeting I was in where the client had expressed that one of our competitors seemed to offer the same services and solutions especially in a specific technology. Within seconds, the lead sales person in the room proceeded to state how that same competitor was not able to accomplish the same things as our technology (giving specific examples). The client listened to the "pitch" then proceeded to state that he disagreed and had personally seen the results given by both companies with no significant differences. The client went on to say that sometimes our company was too arrogant in its approach.

How could that have been done differently? We could have heard what the client had to say and tell him that we would like to conduct some research to ensure all variables and data are being reviewed. The sales lead could have researched the competitive technology and come up with a better response after doing so even though the response may have come days or weeks later. One of the Proverbs states, "Whoever guards his mouth preserves his life; he who opens wide his lips comes to ruin."[80] Understanding when to speak and when not to speak will enable better relationships and reputation. By guarding your mouth or thinking before you speak, you will be able to quell angry responses, ignorant opinions, and arrogant statements (among other benefits).

Be prudent in your communications—apply wisdom before you say anything. Paul wrote to the church at Ephesus, "Let no corrupt communications proceed out of your mouth, but that which is good to the use of edifying, that it may minister grace unto the hearers."[81] When I read this Scripture, I am reminded of one of my favorite television comedies. If you have ever seen *The Andy Griffith Show,* you will know what I am writing about. The lead character, Sheriff Andy Taylor, has a reputation of being a man of integrity, a peacemaker and a loyal friend. Many times throughout years of episodes, Andy speaks with wisdom, love and compassion for his family, his friends and for strangers passing through the town of Mayberry. There literally have been songs written about the simplicity of life in Mayberry. The point is that Andy many times will ensure his communication edifies those around him. He makes sure that his goofy Deputy, Barney Fife, is edified when others put him down (even when Barney made poor decisions).

I remember one episode where Barney had made himself out to be a great wilderness guide. He boasted about learning to live off the land, using nature to guide his way, etc. After leading some boys on a camping trip, he learns that he really is lost and that he cannot light a fire or even catch food. Barney's confidence is shattered and he fears the others will find out the truth. Andy comes to the rescue and without Barney knowing proceeds to put things in place that eventually makes Barney look like the true wilderness guide. Andy starts by first speaking to a friend outside of the campsite and outside of Barney's view. Andy's comments to Gomer were to the edification of Barney. Gomer agrees and proceeds to help Andy carry out his plan of rebuilding Barney's confidence. It worked and Barney regained his confidence and believed he was the wilderness guide and even started bragging again. It is important to note that even when all was said and done and Barney continued to brag, that Andy never said a word about helping.

You may be asking right about now, "so what is the point?" The point is that sometimes we need to think about what our peers may be going through and establish communications that will lift them up at work. And even when they continue to brag about what a wonderful sales rep they are or how many servers they have installed or how many fires they have put out, we continue to edify (truthfully of course). Being slow to speak helps provide better opportunities to do this.

The third statement in the verse is "slow to wrath (or anger)." We must control our anger when we find ourselves getting angry and be very slow to get angry in the first place. Why? Just look at the following verse which states, "For the anger of man does not produce the righteousness of God."[82] The first and foremost reason is that anger does not produce the fruit of the Spirit which is produced through the righteousness of God in one's life. This does not mean there are never proper times to be angry. The Bible states to be angry and sin not.[83] This verse tells us we can be angry, yet the anger must come without sin. Sin would include harmful words to others, selfish intentions of the anger, etc. Paul continues writing in that same verse that we are not to let the sun go down on our anger, meaning resolve it quickly. There are many other Scriptures that deal with anger in the Bible. Several Proverbs provide great insights into the impact of anger and how to deal with anger. One such proverb is that a soft answer turns away wrath.[84] Here is a challenge for you. The next time someone at work is angry (no matter why they are angry) respond with calm words of attention and compassion. You will be amazed at how quickly the anger will fade.

This simple model found in the book of James will go a long way in helping you to be a more effective communicator. Follow these three simple rules: be swift to hear, slow to speak and slow to wrath. Make it a matter of prayer with disciplined practice and you will see results.

The last biblical characteristic for leadership that often goes unnoticed is the ability to act with a sense of urgency. First, let's state what this does NOT mean. It does not mean we are to panic about our business or jobs. It does not mean we make rash decisions for fear of loss of time or result, and it certainly does not mean that all decisions or actions in business require a sense of urgency. What it does mean is that a great leader knows when to "act" with a sense of urgency. All too often I have seen executives in many corporations, as well as first and second level management, react too slowly to a crisis, a trend or simply being slow to achieving results. Great leaders get results. Great leaders communicate a sense of urgency when it is needed and expect their teams to deliver. Leaders must also understand that having a sense of urgency can be a tremendous strength. President Abraham Lincoln stated, "Things may come to those who wait, but only things left by those who hustle." The leaders with a sense of urgency can gain a competitive edge (or mitigate risks) by delivering faster results, moving products to market faster, or by dealing with business issues sooner.

In the book of Revelation,[85] Jesus himself warned the Laodicean church of complacency in their ministry. Instead of being "urgent" about their activities and results, they became complacent and their complacency led to Christ saying, "I will spit you out of my mouth." The background is that Jesus had written letters to several different churches in the book of Revelation.[86] These letters were not only literal to the churches in those specific times but many scholars believe they are also letters to the historical ages of the church with the church of Laodicea being the last age (or the church of the last days before the return of Christ). Christ proceeds to tell the Laodicean church that he knows their works and that they are neither "hot or cold" meaning there was no usefulness to them. Instead, Christ says they are lukewarm Christians and because they are neither hot or cold, he will spit them out of his mouth.[87] This of course is a very strong allegory. He calls them lukewarm because they claim to be rich, increased with many things and have need of nothing. Basically their Christianity was very materialistic and focused purely on earthly things. They had become complacent in the urgent need to disciple and evangelize, two core objectives for every Christian and church. How about you? Have you had a "sense of urgency" to increase in the knowledge of Christ, to grow in the spiritual disciplines and to witness to the lost?

Again, as we apply it to our jobs and workplaces, we need to make sure we are "urgent" about performing well, getting results and being the living example to others.

These biblical characteristics we have covered are not intended to be all-inclusive. There are many other principles and characteristics of leadership we should all pursue and grow in. The intention of this is to get you thinking about different areas of leadership and how the Bible is relevant to those areas. My prayer is that you will continue to study God's word and grow into a transformed Christian which will naturally and spiritually impact all areas of life.

In Summary:

Biblical leadership is often seen as "soft" in its approach. Do you agree with this? Is it true? Why or why not?

_____

_____

_____

_____

Almost every leadership resource states how important integrity is to a leader. Why does the "lack of integrity" still seem to be a major problem in the workplace?

_____

_____

_____

_____

What characteristics do you feel come as a natural strength to you?

_____

_____

_____

_____

What characteristics do you feel are hard to develop? Why?

_____

_____

_____

_____

How will you apply James 1:19 to your life?

_____

_____

_____

_____

How can you be a servant in your workplace?

_____

_____

_____

_____

_____

Why is having a sense of urgency so important?

_____

_____

_____

_____

Sample prayer for guidance on Leadership:

> *Lord Jesus,*
>
> *Thank you for your model and example of servant leadership. Please develop my character to follow after yours. Allow me to make the right decisions in everything that I do. Give me compassion for my peers, my team, and my management. Help me to communicate more effectively. Give me open ears and prudence on when to speak. Enable me to be the best leader I can be while keeping me humble. Use me for your kingdom in my place of work.*
>
> *Amen.*

The Importance of Prudence to Leadership

Webster's (1828 Edition) defines Prudence as: "Prudence implies caution in deliberating and consulting on the most suitable means to accomplish valuable purposes, and the exercise of sagacity in discerning and selecting them." Some people would define Prudence as "having a strong common sense." The word "prudent or prudence" in the KJV is mentioned twenty-eight times. Another inter-relational word used is wisdom which is mentioned 131 times in the Bible. Someone stated that prudence is "wisdom applied to practice." Prudence is the ability to "put all the pieces of a puzzle together" understanding where they fit in business strategy or in life.

It is appropriate that much of our Scripture today is pulled from Proverbs as it is written by King Solomon, the wisest man to have ever lived including present day (his father David was known as a prudent man as well). There are many truths the Bible states about prudence, including prudence must be grounded in light of our relationship with God to be truly effective, and prudence based on our own strength will lead to failure.[88] A prudent leader is constantly seeking knowledge and developing wisdom then consistently practices prudence.[89] A prudent leader invites criticism and reproofs.[90] A prudent leader has the ability to foresee coming issues/problems or opportunities and acts accordingly.[91] Think about these truths for just a minute. Imagine if you were continually seeking knowledge and able to apply to practice. Imagine if instead of cringing or getting annoyed by criticism, you embraced it so that you could learn and grow. Imagine if you had the ability to foresee coming issues or problems and to be able to act accordingly. The flip side of this is that you can foresee coming trends and needs that perhaps you can act on as well. These are biblical truths. They are not subject to Harvard Business Review studies or Wharton MBA analysis. God himself created these truths and they stand firm for eternity.

I have had the opportunity to work with a few prudent people in my life and also in my career; they never cease to amaze me. Many times I have observed these individuals in meetings, events and at social gatherings where they have given the right advice, spoken a calm reply or reacted in just the right way. I know of one individual who seems to not only possess a broad body of knowledge on business, but can also actively participate in the "deep dives" of any one business area. I have been in meetings with him where he is careful in what he says and when he says it. That to me is prudence. How about you? What are the examples of prudence in your life? Do you have a family member, perhaps a grandparent or parent, who is seemingly filled with prudence? If so, how much time do you spend with them? Perhaps you have a friend or co-worker who is prudent? Learn to spend as much with them as you can (with their permission of course).

The real question is how do we develop Prudence? One of the best ways is through experience. Sometimes knowledge (including theory), education, network connections, and technology are not enough. Sometimes the only way to truly learn something is through experience. So naturally if we can learn from experiences, we can significantly grow our knowledge and therefore increase in wisdom allowing us to apply it in prudence. One of the great founding fathers and Christian statesman is Patrick Henry. He was famous for his "… give me liberty or give me death" speech at St. John's Church in Richmond, VA among many other accolades and activities. In a speech to the Virginia Convention on March 23, 1775, Patrick made the following statement regarding experience, "I have but one lamp by which my feet are guided and that is the lamp of experience. I know of no way of judging the future but by the past."[92]

So how do we learn from our experiences? There are many ways. One way is to understand the results of our experiences and capture the strengths and weaknesses leading up to those results. A simple and effective process for this is the After-Action Review (AAR) process. The AAR process is used in the United States Military and other organizations throughout the world. I have adopted the process for use in my own career. The purpose of the AAR is to capture any lessons learned on any completed action, initiative or project. The goal of the AAR process is to enable teams to build improvements for future actions, initiatives or projects, to realize synergies, and to provide benchmarking for peer teams and other organizations. I have adapted my process to include nine major steps.

The first step is to hold an AAR meeting. The participants of the meeting should include those who went through the "first hand" experience as well as others who were customers or perhaps suppliers to the experience (a side note: there should cross-functional representation in this meeting). Also invited should be those teams or individuals that may benefit from hearing the feedback first hand. This meeting is typically thirty to sixty minutes long and strong facilitation is needed. Again, the intent is not to hold a complaint session but a review and improvement session. During this meeting, several core questions are asked and the responses from the group are recorded in the AAR form. After filling out the "experience" information such as project name, purpose of the project, intended goals, etc., the team then proceeds to fill out the rest of the form answering the core questions.

The first question is what were your intended results? This is where the team lists targets, goals, and any other objectives for the action, project or initiative. The second question is what were the actual results? By documenting the actual results, the team can see where the variance is to the intended results. The third question is what caused our results? This is where strong facilitation is needed. Many times the feedback can be very subjective. The group needs to ensure it has all of the data, facts, and any other information related to the project for this AAR. The fourth question is what will we sustain or improve? This is a two part question. Almost every project or experience has something positive about it. The key to learning from experiences is to focus on both positive and negative aspects. Perhaps the experience had great communication even though results were not achieved. It is important to understand what went well. The second part of the question is what will we improve? Formal process communication tools such as brainstorming will help generate ideas for this. The next step in the AAR process is to assign owners and due dates to every action captured in the meeting. You want to ensure there is proper follow-up so the learning is complete. Once the AAR meeting is completed, the team leader (or designated other) can document the results of the meeting on the form and email it to the distribution agreed to. The last step is to celebrate the AAR. There are not many organizations who take the time with a formal process like this and it should be celebrated. Go out to lunch, meet at a Starbucks for afternoon coffee, or if possible have the group recognized in an e-mail or newsletter.

As we have learned, prudence is very important, and biblically there are many truths regarding prudence for our lives. The theologian, Thomas Aquinas, stated, "Prudence is right reason in action." Personally, I love the statement made by the sixteenth President of the United States. Abraham Lincoln once exclaimed, "I do not think much of a man who is not wiser today than he was yesterday." Well said.

In Summary:

Why is Prudence so important for a leader?

_____

_____

_____

_____

_____

Is this a common trait for leaders today? Why or why not?

_____

_____

_____

_____

Why does God think prudence is so important?

_____

_____

_____

_____

Think of a time when you were prudent. How did it make you feel?

_____

_____

_____

_____

Have you been learning new ideas, thoughts or trends within your industry? How?

_____

_____

_____

_____

Do you promote learning with others in your company? How?

_____

_____

_____

_____

What are two things you can do to improve prudence in your life?

_____

_____

_____

_____

Sample prayer for guidance on Prudence:

> *Lord Jesus, my prayer is that you first humble me to realize that without you I am nothing. May you help me to learn from your Word, develop in knowledge to enhance my career, and build my ability to use prudence to be a better child of Christ. May you grant me strength to continue to walk in the path you have chosen for me.*
>
> *Amen.*

Reflection and Leadership

Pulitzer prize winning author David McCullough once stated, "A sense of history is essential to anyone who wants to be a leader, because history is both about people and about cause and effect. History teaches us how to behave in situational variance and shows us how the demands of leadership change from one era to another, from one culture to another."

Why is history so important to leadership and to the marketplace in general? How many research projects or books have been written on the historical performances of companies? Why? Some of the reasons include; to understand benchmarks and strengths, to understand external factors to results, to understand trends, to foresee projections, and to understand weaknesses (SWOT analysis, etc). Invaluable insights come through the historical study and through remembrance of the past. History is just as important to the leader as strategy is. Good leaders learn to look to history in order to develop a more effective future strategy. This is really nothing new.

The Bible is full of Scripture encouraging the reader to learn to reflect, to learn from history and from others who have gone on before. More important, God directs us to remember our past, what He has done for us, and to teach it to future generations. God commanded the nation of Israel that they were to teach "diligently" to their children about what God had done for them as a nation telling them to continually speak of them no matter what activity they were doing or where they were at.[93] Why is this so important? Because God warned they could forget the Lord and his work if they did not remind themselves of it. It is human nature to forget. Think about it. How many times have you forgotten something? Can you remember the goals and strategies for your company last year? Do you recall even the simplest of things from years ago? Who won the World Series ten years ago? Who was President of the United States twenty-five years ago? What was the storyline of your favorite television series on any given date last year? Memory is vital to mankind and without it we would not and could not succeed. One of the best modern books on remembrance and making the most of your place on God's timeline is by Pastor Stu Weber. The book is entitled *Infinite Impact*. In this book, Pastor Stu gives a quote from a 1798 edition of Isaac Watt's volume *The Improvement of the Mind*. The quote states, "So necessary and so excellent a faculty is the memory of man, that all other abilities of the mind borrow from thence their beauty and perfection; for... in a word, there can be neither knowledge, nor arts, nor sciences without memory; nor can there be any improvement of mankind in virtue and morals... without the assistance and influence of this power.... It awakens the dullest spirits."[94] This is a beautiful statement and truth to the importance of memory to humanity.

One of the most important advantages to being a Christian is that the Spirit of God dwells in us no matter where we are and what we are doing. The Holy Spirit communes with each of us, yes, even in the workplace. Have you ever read what Christ stated about the Holy Spirit regarding remembrance? The passage states, "But the *Comforter,* which is the Holy Ghost, whom the Father will send in my name, he shall teach you all things, *and* bring all things to your remembrance, whatsoever I have said unto you."[95] The Holy Spirit will not only teach you all things but will also help you remember the things of Christ as you live daily under his command. This is an important truth. We, as Christians, fail to realize that Christ gave us the solution for a successful relationship with him. By spending time with Christ (in his Word, through worship and prayer) and in the spiritual disciplines (enabling deeper growth in character and relationship), the Holy Spirit will teach us then help us remember what Christ taught us through his Word. As we face the struggles of life, the Holy Spirit will comfort us with memories of the love of Christ. You may be facing a pending layoff, you may have to terminate someone, you may have a daunting deadline or sales goal or you may be "bored" in your job. Rest assured, Jesus knows these struggles too. He understands what it is to manage people, to deal with enemies, to communicate with strangers, to understand timing. By remembering what he has done for us in the past, we will see the future through his lens, and not through our own eyes.

One of the greatest leaders in the Bible was Joshua. He was courageous, loyal and a man of integrity. Joshua received the command to lead the nation of Israel into the promised land upon the death of Moses, his mentor. This required crossing the Jordan River. Once the entire nation had crossed the river, God had an interesting command for Joshua. God told Joshua to gather twelve men, each man representing a tribe of Israel. These men were to go down into the riverbed and pick up twelve large stones. These stones were to be piled together in a memorial. When the children of the men asked what the stones were for, they were to tell them how God led them across the Jordan River into the Promised Land.[96] Why was this story important enough to be written in the Word of God? Pastor Stu Weber writes, "The memorial was not intended to be admired for its human creativity; it was built, straight out of the riverbed, to remind people of their faithful God, who would always carry them, his bride, across every threshold."[97] I believe there is great significance in this story for each of us. Each one of our lives should be filled with "memorials" where we can point people to and say this is what God did for me. That's why it is so important for us to work hard, give our absolute best and work with integrity. These can be "memorials" to our co-workers that we can use to discuss where our strength and wisdom comes from.

We can also learn something else that we can apply to our workplaces. Joshua shows us a model for reflection. I call this model the "Memorial Stones" Cycle. The story of the Memorial stones gives us a basic three step process that God gave to Joshua. Step one was to identify resources to help (the twelve men who were chosen to represent each tribe—this ensured everyone was involved and obeyed). Step two was to retrieve the stones from the Jordan River and set them up for a memorial. Step three was to teach why the stones were there to future generations. Using the same basic approach along with additional elements, we can quickly develop a formal model for use in the workplace. As with all of the processes and tools in this book, the intent is to give you, the reader, alternatives to how you are currently reflecting, or in business terms, "benchmarking" at work. There are many great benchmarking processes used in the marketplace. This simple model is a thought starter for you to consider in your job or at your organization.

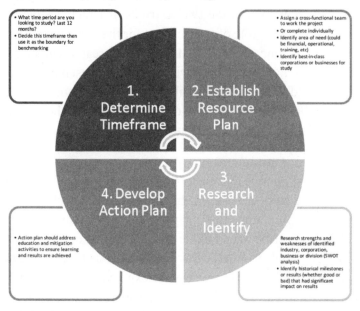

The Memorial Stones Cycle has four basic steps with the assumption that the business need or initiative requiring reflection and benchmarking has been selected. The first step is to *Determine the Timeframe* for which you want to benchmark. This is an important first step. Trends that occurred one hundred years ago may not be relevant for your industry (information technology for example). Sometimes you may only want the last several months as a timeline. This timeframe becomes the start and end boundaries for your benchmarking timeline. With Joshua, God wanted them to remember this "point in time"

which was a significant promise he made to Abraham long before Joshua or Moses were born. Indirectly though, God also was establishing a process for the nation of Israel to remember all that He had done for them right up until the river's edge.

Step Two is to *Establish a Resource Plan*. This resource plan can be anything from individual contributor to a team. If a team, they should be cross-functional where appropriate for cross-pollination of ideas and insights. God told Joshua to gather one man from each of the twelve tribes of Israel. Theologian Matthew Henry wrote of two reasons for the choosing of these twelve men, one from each tribe. The great commentator stated, "One man out of each tribe, and he a chosen man, must be employed to prepare materials for this monument, that each tribe might have the story told them by one of themselves, and each tribe might contribute something to the glory of God thereby."[98]

The first point is that each tribe may have one of their own to relay the story and begin the generational transfer of this knowledge. Accountability plays a key role here. God was holding each tribe accountable to his command. The second point Henry makes is that each tribe might contribute something to the glory of God. There was an expectation, in fact more of a requirement that all tribes participate so that each can contribute to the overall command. You may be asking how does this apply to the workplace or to my job? The answer is simple. When you are looking to benchmark or improve upon something in the workplace, you (and or the team involved) must be accountable for the process and results and all must contribute to be truly effective in driving buy-in to the results. Getting back to the model, other elements of the resource plan include identifying the benchmark or best-in-class processes, departments, organizations, and corporations for your timeline. This is also where you determine if your resources will spend time external to the organization or through internal benchmarking.

One of the business areas I have used this model on is in the area of improving the customer experience (there is a whole chapter devoted to what the Bible says about the customer experience later in this book). I decided to approach this need as an individual and wanted to see what others in business were doing in this area the last year or so. I proceeded to study the latest academic business books on the topic as well as choose two companies to study who were known for their impact on the customer experience albeit in different ways. The first is the Ritz Carlton and the second is Starbucks. My resource plan included books about both companies, internet articles and data mining, and in the case of Starbucks, observation at twenty-five plus stores as I traveled globally. I will explain more as we discover the other two steps in the model.

Step three is *Research and Identify.* Through tools like the SWOT analysis (Strengths, Weaknesses, Opportunities and Threats), the individual contributor or team can research and identify variances, best practices and other pertinent information regarding the business issue or need. One of the best books on creating a customer experience is called *The New Gold Standard* by Joseph A. Michelli. This book is written about the principles the Ritz Carlton Hotel Company uses to create a legendary customer experience. The author writes in detail about the five leadership principles Ritz Carlton uses to train its leaders and employees to be enabled to deliver world class customer experiences. These five principles are Define and Refine, Empower through Trust, It's not about You, Deliver WOW, and Leave a lasting Footprint.[99] I share them here as they became very powerful to me as I worked with my customers around the world. The last principle, "leave a lasting footprint" resonates deeply with me. I want customers to remember their experience with my leadership and services as one of integrity, world-class performance, exceeded expectations, etc. Also, the Bible has plenty to say about making a good name for yourself,[100] good reputations, etc. By researching and learning what others are doing even outside of my industry, I am able to apply lessons learned and other tools to my own experience and leadership style. This is especially true when I travel. At the time of this writing I have almost one million air miles with United and have flown thousands of other miles with other carriers. I have been to many different global cities (some on multiple occasions) including Beijing, Hong Kong, Singapore, Seoul, Tokyo, Mumbai, London, Paris, Zurich and Sao Paulo. During all of this travel I am able to visit different corporations in various cultures. I have found this to be fascinating as I have seen how other cultures engage with customers.

One of the best global companies at maintaining a standard customer experience across global boundaries is Starbucks. I consume more Starbucks than I care to admit; however, what I have found in my travels is that I enjoy going to the "local" Starbucks (I have been to over twenty-five global Starbucks stores and countless stores across the U.S.) for two very important reasons and both have directly impacted my customer experience. The first is that in most cases (of course there is the occasional one, bad tasting cup of coffee but very rare in my opinion), I know I will get a good, consistent cup of strong coffee made to the global standards of Starbucks. The second reason I seek out a Starbucks where I travel is that the store generally gives me a comfortable "I am at home" experience. Due to its ambiance and standard store models, I can feel at home no matter where I am in the world. Sitting at a table in London or Hong Kong with a cup of Sumatra blend, takes me back to stores in the U.S. This of course is my experience and yours may vary. The point is that I have learned from this experience and have tried to apply it to my global customers. I need to be consistent with my delivery standards and processes so that my global customers experience a true global consistency with our products and services. All of this is done through research, benchmarking and simple observation and application methods.

Step four in the Memorial Stones Cycle is to *Develop the Action Plan*. Once you have done your research, benchmarking, and/or other activities, you need to set very clear actions on the next steps. Questions like how are you going to use the information you have collected or how do we apply what we have learned to our department or organization should be asked and answered. Specific actions should be developed with clear ownership and a set timeline for completion. This step is very important and in many cases not often completed, leading to failure. Momentum can only be sustained through movement. You must keep the project moving in order to see sustainable results. This is done through detailed project management and action completion.

All throughout the Bible, reflection upon what God has done is a primary theme. This same theme should be used in our businesses and workplaces. There is nothing wrong with reflecting on what God has done for us in our jobs, careers and workplaces. We are in our jobs for reasons that He is willing to share with us if we let him. Learning through reflection is critical to our success. King Solomon wrote, "Give instruction to a wise man, and he will be yet wiser: teach a just man, and he will increase in learning."[101] The point is that wise men and women continue learning throughout their entire lives. God made us this way. It is his expectation of us. We are to continue learning all we can while keeping him at the forefront and center of all we do. Reflection helps with this.

This chapter started with a very powerful statement from author David McCullough. He states, "A sense of history is essential to anyone who wants to be a leader, because history is both about people and about cause and effect. History teaches us how to behave in situational variance and shows us how the demands of leadership change from one era to another, from one culture to another." History can teach us new strengths, new opportunities, traps to avoid, and how to handle various situations based on the actions of those who have walked the road before us.

There is extremely powerful knowledge in benchmarking (reflection). Understanding what other companies or industries have done right or wrong will enable better decision making based on facts and historical outcomes. The Lord commanded Joshua to set up the Memorial Stones as a reminder to the nation of Israel of what God had brought them through. Sometimes in our lives and careers, it is good to set up the occasional reminder so that we can remember.

In Summary:

Do you know the history of your company? Your employees? Your customers? Your competitors?

_____

_____

_____

_____

_____

Who from history has been an influence on your leadership? On your career? Why?

_____

_____

_____

_____

Why is history so important to God?

_____

_____

_____

_____

Have you read about any historical leaders? What can you share?

_____

_____

_____

_____

Why is it sometimes hard to be accountable?

_____

_____

_____

_____

Reflect on the "Memorial Stones" Model. What do you see as valuable in this model?

_____

_____

_____

_____

Read Joshua 4:1-9. What does this mean to you? Why is this important enough for God to include in His Word?

_____

_____

_____

_____

Sample prayer for guidance on Reflection and Historical Analysis:

> *Lord Jesus,*
>
> *Please help me to remember your laws and your love while engaging in my position and place of work. Teach me to understand what I need to improve in order for me to work in excellence and integrity. Show me where to learn more about my industry, my business, and my customers. In doing so, give me the opportunity to show that I am your child and that through your guidance, I can do all things. Thank you for your grace and for the skills you have given me.*
>
> *Amen.*

A Simple Model for Leadership

Again, let's revisit the definition of "leadership" to ensure we have a solid foundation. As we stated earlier on the chapter, *Webster's 1828 Edition Dictionary defines a leader as: "One that leads or conducts; a guide; a conductor; a commander; a captain." The next definition states "One who goes first." The definition of leading states "showing the way by going first." The modern definition of leadership (Webster's On-Line) is: "The office or position of a leader; capacity to lead; the act or instance of leading."*

Your faith should impact ALL areas of life, including leadership. The model to the right is a simple visual showing the relationship of Faith to family, work and community. Faith should not be relegated to just the

family sphere. If it is, then I would question if the faith is really relevant at all. God is relevant in all of creation, across all cultures and in all industries. Everyone carries their worldview (how they perceive the world) into the workplace and communities they are a part of. Your leadership style also affects every area of your life. Integrating your faith and leadership style can improve your overall character and therefore success. So if faith should impact leadership, what elements of leadership should we focus on according to the Bible?

In order to help the reader remember this model, I have bucketed the core learnings into leadership elements that start with the letter A. This model is not intended to be the all-inclusive model for biblical leadership or for leadership in general. I have found this model to prove very successful in my own career and in the lives of others I have worked with. I encourage the reader to learn all you can about what the Bible says about leadership. I promise you that if you endeavor on such a task with integrity and hard work, you will be rewarded beyond your imagination as we have learned the

Bible contains enormous amounts of wisdom, counsel, and learning.

This model for leadership (what I call "*A*-Model Leadership") enables leaders to learn, grow, get results, and stay true to themselves and others. Each element is built from biblical examples and benchmarking in the marketplace. Balancing *A*-Model Leadership and Spiritual Disciplines (such as studying the Bible, prayer, fasting, etc.) will lead to deeper integration of Faith and Leadership. This is a very important truth that we have highlighted in other areas of this book. Spiritual Disciplines and the practice thereof are the most important activities you can do to improve your life, performance on the job, your leadership, your relationships and your knowledge. You must be willing to read God's word, pray daily, serve others, and reflect in solitude and simplicity. Only in disciplining ourselves in this, can we truly be effective in integrating our faith and work. And by doing this, God will open opportunities you never thought possible.

The first element of *A*-Model Leadership is Authenticity which means true to one's own personality, spirit, or character. It is Integrity in all you do. A recent article in the Harvard Business Review[102] was entitled "How will you measure your life?" by Harvard Business School professor Clayton Christensen. In the article, Professor Christensen outlines how business leaders should be thinking about their lives and not just their careers and how they really should measure success. In a section called "Avoid the Marginal Costs Mistake", he tells the story of how his deep religious faith impacted his basketball career at Oxford University. When he was sixteen, he made a decision (a personal commitment to God) that he would not play basketball on Sundays. Now he was the starting center on the Oxford team and they were facing a "national championship" game on a Sunday. He prayed about it and still felt he should not play. The coach and his fellow players tried talking him out of it by saying, "Can't you break the rule *just this one time?*" He did not break the rule and did not play. He goes on to say, *"In many ways that was a small decision—involving one of several thousand Sundays in my life... but in looking back on it, resisting the temptation whose logic was 'in this extenuating circumstance, just this once, OK' has proven to be one of the most important decisions of my life. Why? My life has been one unending stream of extenuating circumstances. Had I crossed the line that one time, I would have done it over and over in the years that followed."[103]* This is what authenticity is all about. It means to have the courage to be authentic in one's values and beliefs when others disagree and in light of adversity. The Bible says, "if thou faint in the day of adversity, they strength is small."[104] This is a very powerful truth. How do we build up the strength to face adversity? Through spiritual disciplines and being authentic no matter what the cost. Take a moment to reflect on your life. How authentic are you? Do you stand firm in integrity? Or perhaps have you fallen to the "just this once" mentality? Sobering to think about but thinking about it is the first step to improving ourselves.

Authentic leaders breed trust—a required element for success in life. What I have found fascinating and discouraging at the same time is that integrity has been discussed in almost every writing (including research, books and articles) on leadership I have seen. Yet we continue to see how the lack of integrity destroys the reputations of leaders, governments, families and companies, thereby impacting negatively the lives associated with those entities such as spouses, children, citizens, employees, customers and suppliers, not to mention shareholders. Why is this? I believe it is because we are trying to base our integrity on man-made objectives and not on God's law. It is easy for the Christian to recognize that we as humans are subject to a sinful nature. It is the very reason we accepted Christ as our personal Lord and Savior. We understand that without Christ in our lives, sin will remain in control, period. There is no exception to this truth. So in trying to establish cultures of integrity within our families, governments, and workplaces without recognizing human nature for what it is (sinful), we "gloss" over a root cause that eventually comes out in one form another (greed, dishonesty, fraud, abuse, etc). We must be authentic in our personal lives founded upon God's principles if we are truly to lead with authenticity.

The Bible is very clear on being a person of authenticity and where that authenticity comes from. Daniel was an Authentic leader.[105] In the first chapter of the book of Daniel, Daniel and other Jews were held captive in Babylon. Daniel was with the group selected by king Nebuchadnezzar because they were brilliant young men with many skills. The custom was to train these young men in the ways of Babylon and have them serve the king. Part of the ritual was to have the young men partake in the dietary regiment of the king, including meat. However, this diet was a defilement of Jewish law and Daniel wanted no part of it. The King James Version of the Bible states that Daniel "purposed" in his heart that he would not defile himself...

The word purposed in Hebrew is *suwm or siym* which are root words meaning to put, to determine, to purpose, to resolve, to set upon among other applications. Daniel was determined to be authentic in his faith. He was *resolved* not to take the meat as the ESV puts it. Because Daniel was a man of integrity and authenticity, God provided favor and strength (v. 9). This same authenticity got Daniel into trouble later in his life. His competitors, jealous of his leadership and integrity, tricked the king of that time (Darius) to establishing a law that no one may pray or communicate with any god or man for thirty days except to King Darius. The law in and of itself was ridiculous but there was a reason. The enemies of Daniel had tried to find other faults (perhaps a dishonest business dealing or false accounting on his taxes, etc.) and could not do so. Why? Because Daniel was a man of integrity. He was authentic. The Bible says he was faithful. So they created a law that would attack his integrity because they knew he would be authentic to his God. Daniel prayed everyday consistently and these enemies knew this. The law basically made it illegal (by penalty of death in the lions den) to pray. Now some Christians may have justified not praying by saying "its only thirty days, I can resume after that" or "I will hide what I do so they will not know I am still doing it." Both of these responses would have destroyed the authenticity of Daniel and he knew it. He chose to pray to God anyways.

What can we learn from this story and how can we apply it to our work lives? First, we must resolve ourselves into living for God in the workplace no matter what trials, peer pressure, harassment or temptations we face. Is your life "different" in the workplace? Do you participate in the "favorite dirty joke of the week" discussion or perhaps drink excessively when at business functions? Do you take office supplies home because "it's only a pen?" Do you cut corners in production or manufacturing to improve the bottom line knowing quality is impacted? Do you call in sick when you are not really sick? Do you gossip about other peers or your boss? Do you "step on others" while trying to climb the ladder? Is your marketing or advertising campaign honest? I recently heard a commercial on a Christian radio station where the radio show host had "claimed to send an e-mail to a friend promoting the services of a law firm." The radio show host (a Christian I presume) then read the e-mail he sent to his friend. One could easily tell due to the language of the e-mail that he would not have sent this e-mail phrased the way it was phrased. It was clear the campaign was made to "look" like the host was recommending the services. I find this questionable from an integrity standpoint.

We must determine to live as God would have us live. Authenticity is not always easy, but it is always right. Secondly, we must strive to be the best performers at work while also encouraging our peers to be at their best. We must seek God's purpose for our work and ask for his direction and favor so that we can be used by him. Daniel was used in the workplace. He was not used in church. May our fellow co-workers make the same statement of us that Daniel's co-workers said of him; "we shall not find any ground for complaint against this Daniel unless we find it in connection with the law of his God."[106] The Bible says to come out from among them and be ye separate. Do others see a difference in you?

The second element of *A*-Model leadership is Awareness. Awareness implies vigilance in observing or alertness in drawing inferences from what one experiences. Prudence and Awareness go hand in hand. One of the great proverbs states, "a prudent man foreseeth the evil, and hideth himself; but the simple pass on, and are punished."[107] A Christian who is aware of their surroundings, their relationships, and their walk with God will be able to avoid much of the trouble in life. This applies to work as well. Awareness of industry trends may help us get further educated on areas we would not have known about if we were "not aware."

Throughout my leadership career, I have seen many people fail in their roles because they were not "aware" of pending shifts in technology or a change in strategic direction. In fact, I believe that one of the strongest ways to avoid being laid off, burnt-out or bored with your job is to remain relevant to the business. Notice I did not say relevant to the position. High performance and relevance will keep anyone employed for their careers. Even if somehow they are laid off, they will not be unemployed for long.

Part of the reason is awareness. These same high performers will be aware of opportunities and take advantage of networks, etc. Leaders who build awareness skills enable themselves to be better prepared in life. Awareness should drive action. Awareness includes understanding trends, personalities, strategies, competition, opportunities, morale, etc.

Mordecai was a leader who was aware.[108] When his niece Esther was queen to king Ahasuerus, enemies of the Jews arose and convinced the king to establish a decree to destroy all of the Jews on a set date. Esther herself was a Jew and this was unknown to the king and others. Mordecai kept himself informed of all matters and worked with Esther to formulate a plan where the Jews were to fast and lament until the hour Esther would present herself to the king and ask for a reversal. Mordecai was a Jew and a man of God. He stayed true to the Lord and worked diligently to serve him in all he did. Through his awareness of his surroundings and his relational networks, Mordecai was able to thwart the plan of Haman and his enemies (make no mistake, God's hand was on Mordecai and Esther and through his intervention they were saved). The point here is that Mordecai and Esther took action through their awareness. Awareness is one piece of the puzzle. As psychologist Phil McGraw states, "Awareness without action is worthless."

"Do you want to know who you are? Don't ask. Act! Action will delineate and define you," stated Thomas Jefferson, third President of the United States. Action is the third element of *A*-Model leadership and can be defined as accomplishment of something, usually over a period of time, in stages, or with the possibility of repetition. Real leaders get results through effective action. Strategies are ineffective without action. Battle plans are useless without action. This is true in the spiritual realm as well. Spiritual warfare requires spiritual action. No action on the part of a Christian results in complacency, compromise and eventually destruction. Taking action at work, at home, at church, at school and in life in general will lead to greater success. I have worked with people who got things done and with those who talked a lot about getting things done. The difference is those who executed were high performers and many were promoted, rewarded and/or recognized consistently. The management of actions is a crucial skill. No matter what job you are in, execution of your work is critical to your success. Mail carriers need to deliver their routes accurately and on-time. Baristas at Starbucks need to create drinks with quality and speed. Contractors need to build according to plans and on schedule. Fire fighters need to arrive quickly and perform with skill. Sales reps need to close the sale with quality and timeliness (quotas). All of these have three common denominators. The first is they all have to execute certain actions to achieve their goals. Secondly, they must do the job right. And thirdly they must do it with speed. A leader who knows how to drive execution balanced with quality and speed is a successful leader.

David was a leader of action.[109] There are many examples of the great leadership of David and how he executed many actions enabling success for the nation of Israel and himself. The story that stands out and provides a great illustration is the story of how he defeated the giant Goliath. The nation of Israel was frozen in fear as Goliath stood before them. Saul, the king of Israel, and his armies had set up across the valley from the armies of the Philistines but that's as far as they went. No other action was taken. Goliath, a nine foot, nine inch monster of a man (a full two feet taller than future NBA hall of fame center Shaquille O'Neal) had come out across the valley and challenged Israel to a one on one battle with their best soldier. As he cursed Israel and their God, he defiantly requested a winner take all death match. If Goliath won, Israel would serve the Philistines. If the nation of Israel won, then the Philistines would serve Israel.

Goliath was very intimidating to look at. His armor coat weighed 125 pounds. The spear head of his spear was over 15 pounds of iron. He was a proven battle champion and I am sure the nation of Israel had heard his name before. Saul and the nation of Israel were greatly dismayed and full of fear states the Bible. As leader, Saul's job was to accept the challenge of Goliath and take action to meet him. He did neither. In the meantime, David, a shepherd boy by trade, was sent by his father to the Israeli army camp to check on the welfare of his brothers who were serving Saul as soldiers. After arriving in the camp, David overhears the curses and challenge coming from Goliath.

David becomes angry and begins to hear the men discuss how whoever kills Goliath will reap rewards from king Saul. David responds and asks what will the man receive that kills this Philistine? For who is this uncircumcised Philistine that he should defy the armies of the living God? There are three things we can apply to are own lives and leadership. The first is David gets clarification on the goal. He asks what shall be the reward of killing this Philistine? Secondly, David has already assumed action is needed. David was a man of action. He was not about to stand around and listen to this Philistine anymore. He already knew that he must kill Goliath. Thirdly, David lived with authenticity. He was a man of God who loved the Lord (in fact David is written as being a man after God's own heart). He knew the real issue at stake. He understood that Goliath was defying the armies of the *living God.* This same God will deliver David.

Saul gets word about David's reaction and calls him to the front. David proceeds to tell Saul that he is experienced with dealing with crisis such as this and that God had helped him in those times and will certainly do so again.[110] Saul agrees to let him challenge Goliath. After declining to use Saul's armor, David goes with what he is experienced with and that is the sling and stones. As David approaches, Goliath disdains him and curses at him stating he will feed him to the birds. David responds by stating, "...I come to thee in the name of the Lord of hosts, the God of the armies of Israel whom thou hast defied. This day will the Lord deliver thee into mine hand... for the battle is the Lord's and he will give you into our hands." David runs towards Goliath as Goliath comes towards him and slings a stone deep into the forehead of Goliath knocking him to the ground unconscious. David takes the sword of Goliath and uses it to cut off the head of his enemy.

So you may be asking, how do I apply this story? What can I learn from David? I would like to point out five additional truths from this story that we can apply to our lives as leaders. The first truth is that David "remembered" what God had done in the past and was confident in his faith that God would deliver him again. God has done significant things in all of our lives yet how often we forget. Instead, when the next crisis comes along, we act as if we have never received support from God and panic. We need to remember God when we face all of our trials, issues, problems and challenges. This includes the workplace. God cares about the looming deadline, or pending layoff, or angry co-worker. He understands days-sales-outstanding and how it impacts your bottom line. He knows when your manager is mistreating you. He understands the pressure of the Board and company shareholders and what you need for peace. Remember what he has done and rely on his support once again. He will never fail you.

The second truth is that David relied on the experiences God gave him. David knew the sling and stone. He had proved them in protecting his father's flock. Saul had offered his armor but David did not feel right in it. Sometimes people will throw ideas and opinions our way and we become caught up in the way they have done it. We need to stand firm in what we know to work and stay focused. Learning from others in and of itself is not necessarily wrong (in fact it should be encouraged). However, in times of crisis, we need to rely on tested principles to get us through. The third truth we can apply is that David relied directly on God's support even though he was skilled and experienced. We as leaders and Christians at work need to rely more on the wisdom of God through prayer and less on our own skills and abilities. That is not very politically correct but it is true. Imagine if every Christian really prayed fervently for their performance, their co-workers and their companies. It would be a different world. The fourth truth is that David ran towards the problem, not away from the problem. Leaders need to be proactive and sometimes aggressive when dealing with problems, challenges or pending issues. In doing so, much of the problem can be mitigated before too much damage is done, if any. It will also build confidence in your peers and fellow co-workers. The fifth truth is that action was needed by someone and David took it. Sometimes leaders need to take the first action to get something done. Sometimes leaders need to show action to motivate teams.

Agility is marked by ready ability to move with quick, easy grace and/or having a quick, resourceful and adaptable character. Leaders need to be able to see change and act upon it with effectiveness and efficiency. The ability to be agile in leadership can separate success and failure. Agility enables stronger change management. The apostle Paul was a leader with agility.[111] Throughout his ministry, Paul was able to understand the cultures he was in and be agile enough to shift his approach in ministry. In the book of Acts, we are told of a time when Paul was preaching in Greece. The background is that Paul was sent to Athens to avoid Jewish persecution where he was waiting on Silas and Timothy to join him. While he was waiting, Paul was "stirred in his spirit" as he saw the idolatry of the Athenians. He began to debate with the Jews in the synagogue there and in the marketplace where others met with him to debate his doctrine. This caught the attention of many philosophers (no surprise as it was Greece). He was asked to elaborate on the doctrine he was speaking about. From Mars Hill, Paul delivered a critical sermon on God as judge through Jesus Christ. Mars Hill was famous for philosophical debates and Socrates, Plato and Aristotle had all debated there. Paul opened the sermon by telling them that while he was walking around beholding the objects of their worship he had noticed a tomb with an inscription that read "to the unknown god." He went on to say that though they were ignorant of God, he would declare God unto them. What followed is a beautiful sermon on God, Christ and the relationship with man apart from objects or man-made idols.

There are several points we can learn from Paul and his agility when dealing with the people of Athens. The first point is that Paul, being filled with Christ, was stirred in his spirit due to the sin in Athens. Are we "stirred" in our workplaces when we see others suffering or sinning? Are we filled with the knowledge and righteousness of Christ to where we are able to sense when things are wrong? The second point is that Paul made it a point to understand the culture in Athens. He walked around and noticed what their beliefs were. He saw firsthand their idols. In doing so this allowed him to speak to their needs (agility). In our day to day lives, do we anticipate the changes that come along, and how agile are we when dealing with them? There are obvious times that require sudden agility. Meetings get changed, customers have emergency requests, or travel delays cause schedule changes. We either learn to be quickly agile or we become bitter, frustrated and/or impassioned. There are also times where agility can be planned for so that when the time comes we are ready. A sales solution with multiple options goes a long way in closing a deal versus too much focus on one option even when we truly believe the option is the best one.

The third and final point is that Paul's agility to preach to the Athenians resulted in new converts. He got results. Agility should be for the sole purpose of getting results. There should be no other reason to be agile. We change our approach, our tactics, or our strategies to accommodate factors that were not considered or in play when we first started out. We only do so to achieve results. The ability to be agile in life and in leadership is only successful if the change resulted in objectives being met. Starbucks learned this the hard way. Their leadership had decided it was time to be agile to competition, new consumer demands and volatile markets. Different products were introduced and changes to the customer experience were made. This resulted in negative growth and a loss of market share. Starbucks had to change leadership and Howard Schultz, the Founder, was brought back in as CEO. Schultz and the team recognized that Starbucks had lost its original vision and immediately Schultz took two actions that some thought were crazy. The first action is that he flew 10,000 store managers to New Orleans for community service and a leadership conference for a week. The second action is that he closed all stores for a mandatory four hour training session. Both of these actions were done with and through agility. Starbucks leadership was agile enough to realize they needed a fast change in core vision education. It came with very high costs, but already Starbucks is seeing a rebound in market share and sales.[112] A leader's ability to be agile when needed is critical to success in life.

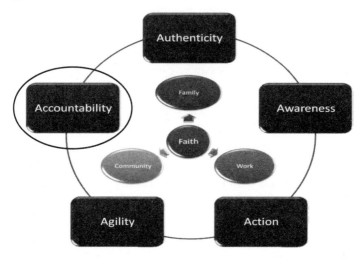

The fifth element of *A*-Model leadership is Accountability. Accountability is defined as the quality or state of being accountable; an obligation or willingness to accept responsibility or to account for one's actions. Accountable leaders create accountable cultures. Over the last few decades, we have seen an unprecedented number of corporations and individual leaders fall to some form of crime, greed, immorality or dishonest action. The sheer arrogance of some of these firms and leaders was mind-boggling. We heard how employees of Enron were recorded as saying "they hope fires continue burning—burn baby burn" as they continues to make a fortune on others' misfortunes. Traders, politicians, and others indicted on fraud and other charges. Let me ask you a question. What is the difference between this activity and the activities done by thousands of people every day when they write off so-called "business expenses" due to loopholes? The same behavior is exhibited. It's called compromise. One of the primary ways to eliminate compromise and unethical behaviors is to establish accountability in your leadership and life. Accountability fosters humility and deflates pride. Pride goes before destruction as the Bible says. I have served under many leaders who were bold in being accountable to their mistakes and that of the company. I have also seen other leaders rely on every excuse to place the blame elsewhere.

Joseph was a leader who knew how to be accountable. He knew he was accountable to God first and foremost.[113] Even during the daily advances of Potiphar's wife (who was very beautiful), Joseph maintained his integrity. Why? I believe the answer lies in the response Joseph gives to the wife. Joseph stated how could he commit this sin against his God? Joseph was accountable to God and took that accountability seriously. I also believe that Joseph felt accountable to Potiphar and others in his life but first to his God. God expects us to be accountable for our actions.

As a Christian and perhaps a leader in your career, are you accountable? Do you promote accountability at work? Do you enable peers, employees, customers, suppliers, partners, etc. to be accountable to their mistakes without ridicule? I remember hearing the story of one manager who said, "I don't care how many mistakes you make so long as each mistake is made farther apart in time from the last mistake you made." In other words, fewer and farther between. We all know mistakes and bad decisions will happen. We need to own them, learn from them and grow from them. If we own, learn and grow from each sin, mistake or bad decision, we will be much better people for it. You can start by opening up to someone you trust. Tell them about the issue at hand and ask them to hold you accountable. At first this may be difficult to do. You may be embarrassed, hurt, angry, or depressed. If your accountability partner (mentors can play this role) truly cares for your well being, they will certainly be glad to listen to you and encourage you along the way.

In review, Leadership is an awesome responsibility. If we are granted such a responsibility, shouldn't we do whatever it takes to become better at it? Authentic leaders build trust—a key element in any team or organization. *A*-Model leadership uses an objective source (God's Word) to improve on secular business leadership. Leadership gets results. Period. Take action! Admit your challenges, your failures and your fear. Then improve upon them. Be accountable. In working on these elements of leadership and in combination with practicing the spiritual disciplines, you will become the leader and Christian worker God has called you to be.

In Summary:

Why was Daniel so successful at being authentic, especially in his Governmental role?

_____

_____

_____

_____

_____

A key step for building awareness is learning. What specific things can you do to increase your learning on the job?

_____

_____

_____

_____

_____

What actions have you procrastinated on at work? How can you get those done? Develop a plan.

_____

_____

_____

_____

_____

_____

Are you good with change? How do you manage change?

_____

_____

_____

_____

_____

Why is it sometimes hard to be accountable?

_____

_____

_____

_____

_____

The apostle Paul was able to be agile when speaking at Mar's Hill. What can better agility do for your job or company?

_____

_____

_____

_____

_____

Of the five elements of *A*-Model Leadership, which element do you struggle with and why? What can you do to improve in that element?

_____

_____

_____

_____

_____

Sample prayer for guidance on Leadership:

> *Lord Jesus,*
>
> *Thank you for your model and example of servant leadership. I ask you to give me strength, courage and wisdom to become a better leader. Help me to be authentic to your Word and stand in integrity. Increase my learning so that I may take the proper actions in my work or career position and in life. Let me understand change for what it is and enable me to manage through change with strong agility. Please keep me accountable in everything I do and may I keep you first in all areas of my life.*
>
> *Amen.*

Chapter 4

Biblical Relevance to the Customer Experience

One of the most important areas for any business is what their customers experience with their products and/or services. A bad customer experience leads to exponential problems and bad publicity. A great customer experience provides value to both the customer and the business enabling the company to have a competitive advantage over time.

But what is the customer experience? One simple definition could be any feeling, emotion, and/or result brought on by interactions with any touch-point of a company's process, products or services. Contributors to Wiki.org have defined it as, "Customer experience is the sum of all experiences a customer has with a supplier of goods or services, over the duration of their relationship with that supplier. It can also be used to mean an individual experience over one transaction; the distinction is usually clear in context." We all have had customer experiences, both good and bad as defined by our standards. An example of a great customer experience I had recently was on a cooler than normal summer Sunday afternoon in Lower Manhattan (New York City). I had arrived at the Marriott Downtown across from the World Trade Center site fresh off of a cross-country flight. In town for business, I was looking forward to getting to my room for some relaxation prior to an early Monday start. The doorman greeted me very nicely welcoming me to the Marriott.

I really thought nothing much of it as I have been greeted like that by hundreds of doormen over the years. It was after I went out for dinner and was walking back, I finally realized the customer experience this doorman was providing. As I walked up to the front of the hotel, he greeted me with a smile and said, "There he is again, welcome back sir." This may seem small to you but I suddenly realized he was paying attention to his guests. I was important enough for him to remember. I am loyal to Marriott because of many examples like this throughout my global travels. This is truly what world-class customer experience is all about. Imagine if every employee in your company or business treated customers with dignity, compassion, caring, and a servant's heart. Your profits, your revenues and your market share would climb.

As we study biblical principles around the customer experience, let's keep three central truths in mind regarding your customers. The first truth is: Customers are more than a means to an end (revenues, profits). This is very difficult to grasp for many businesses as we all want to make profits (and should as that is one of the primary reasons of business). However, customers are people made in the image of God according to the Bible and this itself is revolutionary in current business theory and practice. By believing in the dignity of every customer and providing honest value to each one of them, a business will go a long way in establishing a sustainable long-term strategy.

The second truth is that customers will not remain uninformed for long. The fast growth of information on demand (internet, social media sites, networks, etc.), has allowed the customer to communicate faster than ever and in parallel gain knowledge on businesses faster than ever. Assuming your customer does not know your businesses' strategy or objectives is planning for eventual failure.

The third and final truth is that a customer's perception of your services is their reality, whether you agree or not. Until you change their perception, you will not change their "reality" of your business. I have heard debate about this statement but frankly I don't understand how you can think otherwise. While I realize my bad experiences with a company may not be the overall reality of how they do business, the simple fact remains that I have had bad experiences with them which leads to loss of my business. Marshall Field once said, "Right or wrong, the customer is always right." This includes any misconceptions or perceptions about your business.

There are many great books, methodologies and tools available for understanding, developing and improving the customer experience for your workplace. Articles in Harvard *Business Review, Wall Street Journal,* and other periodicals are great resources in better understanding this critical area. One of the goals of this book is to give the reader simple business tools and methodologies as well as biblical principles to enhance their development and performance in different business areas.

During my career, I have had the privilege of working on customer experience strategies and below is a simple model I helped to develop for a national business:

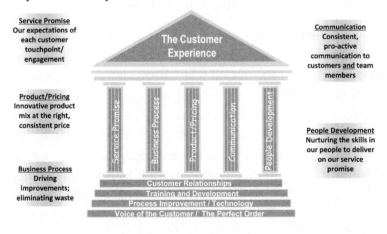

We found the Parthenon Model approach easy to develop (with a lot of research, data collection and benchmarking behind it). Let me briefly explain the foundational steps, the pillars, and the roof. The customer experience (for this company) focused on four key foundational steps (these steps may be different for your company). We wanted to implement a formal voice of the customer feedback system for every area of our supply chain including billing. We used process improvement methodologies and tools to understand gaps. Our goal was to formally train each one of our team members on what the customer experience is and how they impact it in their jobs, so developing a training program was foundational. We also wanted to leverage the great customer relationships we had and use those to improve others. These became foundational for our pillars and needed to be solid for our success.

The pillars are what directly sustain the customer experience (roof). The model briefly describes each pillar. As stated earlier, this is a simple model but can be very effective with proper development and execution. Now that we have explored some business learning in this area, lets take a look at what the Bible can teach us about the customer experience.

The Customer Experience and the Bible

The Bible is filled with Scriptures about relationships of every kind. Many of these Scriptures are very relevant for your customers. The Word of God is also filled with actionable steps to improve one's character and customer service skill-set. There are six biblical principles (what we call the CE6 Principles for memory sake) that we will discuss. Three of them are relational and three of them are action-oriented. As we progress, remember that the more you practice spiritual disciplines (reading the Bible and praying daily, fasting, solitude, serving, simplicity, etc.), the better business professional you will be and your customer's experience with you will improve (this is a guarantee).

The CE6 principles are the Image, Honesty, Pay-Forward, Knowledge, E910, and Servant Principles. As you read about these, try to picture situations in your current workplace where these might have an impact. Later, at the end of this chapter, you will be asked some questions for reflection as well.

The Image Principle—In the Book of Genesis, it states that God created man (and woman) in his own image and blessed them.[114] Theologically, this is a very strong Scripture with enormous meaning, of which we cannot delve deeply into as it is outside the purpose of this writing. However, the principle is very pertinent. If God created all humans in His image, then this includes your customers. And if God loves each and every one of us because He created us then this also includes your customers.[115] By recognizing and believing that all humans are made in the image of God, we should have a new perspective on each human being including the customer. This individual is made in the image of God and is loved by Him. If we truly believe this, then we would treat every client with respect, dignity and with love.

The Honesty Principle—In two specific letters to two different churches (the church in Rome and in Thessalonica), the apostle Paul writes very short, concise commandments about honesty and integrity. To the church at Rome (and subsequently to us) he wrote, "...provide things honest in the sight of all men."[116] This statement contains nine words in total yet its impact, if followed, is very powerful. Imagine your company providing honesty in everything they do. Can you think of examples of corporations who are known for this quality? There are not many that I can think of.

By acting honestly with your customers, you build their trust in you and your business. With growing trust, comes growing confidence. A customer who has confidence in you will become a loyal customer. Sometimes always being honest can be very difficult and may result in a loss of business. Unfortunately, not all customers are honest. Fortunately, God will honor you and your business overall by following this principle consistently. To the church at Thessalonica, Paul wrote, "abstain from all appearance of evil."[117] This has even deeper meaning. It means we are to not even look like we are being dishonest even when we are not. Why is this so important? Because perception is reality in human nature. If a customer perceives you are dishonest, then they will most likely assume it to be true until proven otherwise (a process you want to avoid at all costs). So what can we do? Always be transparent with your customer (of course there are times of confidentiality, etc. when you cannot tell your customer anything, but even then tell them you can't and why). This one seems to be a "no-brainer" yet for many people it is very difficult to manage. They would rather drive sales/profits a little higher by being a little less honest or hide issues from the customer to conduct "damage control" when in fact once the client uncovers it, now the real damage has occurred in the breaking of trust.

The Pay-Forward Principle—Read Matthew 7:12 (also known as the Golden Rule). Matthew writes "therefore all things whatsoever ye would that men should do to you, do ye even so to them..." If you ever went to Sunday School, you probably were taught this Scripture multiple times over. Let's apply it from a customer perspective. If you treat your customers with the same service you would expect from a business or service, then you are well on your way to establishing a great customer experience. Why? Because you wouldn't want a bad customer experience yourself. God wants us to treat everyone as we would want to be treated. The best way to start doing this is by viewing your business from the customer's viewpoint. Get out and touch all of the points a customer would normally touch with your business

The Knowledge Principle—King Solomon wrote, "the fear of the Lord is the beginning of knowledge: but fools despise wisdom and instruction."[118] If you learn anything from this writing, learn this principle. It all starts with an awesome reverence of God. When we surrender all areas of our life including our jobs to Him, He can then begin to build our character, bless our life, and grow us into His purpose and plan for each one of us. Once that is realized, you can then begin to really develop yourself in line with God's direction for your life. There are two other points regarding this principle. Proverbs 23:12 says to apply your heart unto instruction, and your ears to the words of knowledge. Proverbs 15:22 states without counsel purposes are disappointed... The first point is that we should fully apply our lives to learning with all our hearts. The second point is that we need the wise counsel of others to continue to learn the right way to do things.

"Real" leadership never stops learning. Knowledge building, practicing the use of wisdom and prudence, and obtaining counsel (benchmarking, focus groups and other feedback loops) will all help improve the customer experience.

The E910 Principle—Ecclesiastes 9:10 states "whatsoever is in your hand, do with all your might..." This is a direct recommendation from the wisest man to have ever lived. One of the main reasons is that we only have one chance at life. What we choose to decide and take action on can only happen during this lifetime. Why not strive to be your best? God expects us to work as unto Him as we have already explored.[119] Always strive for excellence in everything you do. You must foster an environment of high performance to achieve world-class customer experience. Another key to success is to maintain this principle even when your business is flourishing.

How do you strive to be your best? In three simple steps. Pray for God's wisdom in your life, continue learning (the Knowledge Principle), and take action/get results. In giving God the glory and asking for His guidance, He will prepare your heart and mind for learning (at times you will be amazed at how fast or at what capacity you have learned by praying). The next step is to continue learning to improve your skills and knowledge. Start by understanding your customer's industry and that of your own company. You should also network with many resources, cross-functionally and across industries. Finally, take some action and drive results. All too often we see leaders stall in this area for fear of risks, lack of decision-making confidence, complacency, etc. Real leaders get results, period. Consider the parable of the talents that Christ told.[120] In this story, three different people are given money to invest while the master is away. Two of the three people took action and received double the interest on their investments. The last person took no real action and instead for fear of risk, held on to the original sum. When the master returned, he *expected* results (A quick side note here is that there is nothing wrong with leaders expecting results). The person who took no action was disciplined. As I look at all of the leaders globally I have had the privilege to work with in companies like Xerox, Goldman Sachs, BlackRock, Home Depot, HSBC, JP Morgan Chase, Bank of America, and many non-profits, I can quickly call to mind those that were known for delivering results versus those who had opportunity in this area.

If your customer truly saw that you were among the best in your industry, it would go a long way in developing a solid foundation for the overall customer experience.

The Servant Principle—Read Mark 12:28-31. As stated in another chapter, there have been many business books touting the positive results a leader can have when applying servanthood principles. This is nothing new as Jesus demonstrated this time and time again over 2,000 years ago. Imagine if your customer truly felt like you were serving their needs. What does that look like you may be asking? What steps have you taken to ensure you are serving your customer? Have you asked them for their pain-points? Or what makes them "lose sleep at night?" Have you discussed their likes and dislikes? Have you given them value on as service or product without asking for something in return?

One of the things I like to do when I think about my customer base is to ask myself, if one of my competitors or company leaders had a meeting with my client and asked them if they felt I was serving their needs and business, what do I think the customer would respond with? Sometimes in thinking through this thought process (and being fully honest in our assessments) we may find nuggets of information that we can act upon.

The CE6 Principles are designed for you to think about how the Bible interacts with the customer experience and what you need to think and do to help understand your customers better. The next logical question is how do we improve the customer experience? In the following pages, we will be discussing a simple closed-loop cycle with the goal of getting you to understand various ways to improve the customer experience in your business.

The EPL Customer Experience Improvement Model

Peter Drucker wrote, "The single most important thing to remember about any enterprise is that there are no results inside its walls. The result of a business is a satisfied customer." At Eagle Peak Leadership, we have developed a simple model based on research and benchmarking across multiple industries and resources. This model is not intended to be the "end-all" model nor is it the only effective model for improving the customer experience. Our intention is to give you a starting point so that you can begin to think about what you would need to improve the CE for your business.

By reviewing this model, the hope is that you will learn about what areas of your business to look at to impact and improve the customer experience. Smart companies understand their customer's experiences with their services or products so they can improve upon them faster than the competition. As you reflect on the EPL CE Improvement Model, think about your own customer experiences and where some of the companies you have done business with may have improved.

The CE Improvement Model focuses on four specific elements for improving the customer experience of your company. Eagle Peak has researched many top global and multi-national corporations to understand how they have improved their customer experiences. This model is meant to be simple. Understanding our customers should start with the basics of human interaction. The four key elements are Principle, People, Planning and Precision. There are also four Gap Closure Factors (GCFs). Gap Closure Factors are specific characteristics or areas of relationships, development and results that can "close the customer experience gap" for a respective element.

It all begins with *Principle.* According to the three relational principles defined by the Bible (The Image Principle, The Honesty Principle and the Pay-Forward Principle), we are to treat our customers with dignity, with honesty, and as we would expect to be treated if we were customers. We have all seen poor treatment of employees, customers, suppliers and shareholders. There are also three action principles (The Knowledge Principle, The E910 Principle and the Servant Principle) where according to the Bible, we are to develop ourselves beginning with the Knowledge of God, do everything within our grasp with excellence, and serve others. Companies and Organizations with great reputations for standing on principles (whether you agree with their principles or not) include Federal Express and the United States Marine Corps. The GCF for Principle is Integrity. Without integrity, your principles will fail. If your principles fail, your business will ultimately fail. We have all been reminded of this with the recent global economic crisis in 2008 and 2009 where many financial institutions and individual leaders failed to stand on principles. Companies like Bear Stearns, WaMu, Lehman

Brothers, etc. were quickly swallowed up by competition due to lack of principles in the way they did business. The entire world was affected. Businesses from Beijing to Bangalore, from Tokyo to Toronto, from London to Los Angeles were all affected. Unemployment rates skyrocketed as the economic failures were exposed. In the U.S., unemployment reached greater than 10 percent, a number not seen in decades. In Spain, unemployment rates hit greater than 14 percent.

Principles are vital to successful business and they are vital to your customer experience. Your customer must believe your business operates with integrity in order for them to "really" partner with you.

The second element of focus in the Improvement Model is *People*. It has been said, "Take care of your people and they will take care of your customers." Do you believe this? Why or why not? So often companies lose sight of their employees and the value they bring to the organization. The better your employees are respected, developed, recognized and rewarded, the higher the confidence your customers will have in your business. Extreme confidence leads to world-class customer satisfaction and experience. A prime example of this is the Ritz-Carlton Hotel Company. They pride themselves on the treatment and development of their people. It shows in their customer service which reflects nicely in the experiences of their customers. Xerox Corporation, Fuji-Xerox (Asia), Enterprise Car Rentals, and Starbucks are other great business examples.

The Gap Closure Factor for the area of People is confidence. You need to build the confidence in your customers that your employees, partners, and suppliers are working to the level of excellence they desire. Customers want to see people who understand the business. They want to feel confident that your representatives are looking out for the best interests of the customer and not the bottom line and/or compensation plans.

The third element of focus for the CE Improvement Model is *Planning*. Planning incorporates the organization's overall strategic plan and the tactical plans tied to the strategic plan. There have been many books written on this topic and many more companies profess to have a great planning process. But do they really? Can an organization's planning process ever really be "foolproof?" Throughout the history of work, we have seen plans fail in all industries. The planning process must have the customer experience in mind. An organization's core strategy must directly influence the customer experience.

The Gap Closure Factor for Planning is knowledge. Companies and Organizations who take the time to listen, benchmark, and to study their customers and industry trends will ultimately beat out their competition and increase market share. Steve Jobs, CEO of Apple, once stated, "You can't just ask customers what they want and then try to give that to them. By the time you get it built, they'll want something new." This quote is very true. Knowledge and the obtainment of it, is at its core.

The fourth and final element is that of *Precision*. Have you ever been to an air show where there was a military pilot team performing? I have had the privilege of watching the Blue Angels Navy Performance Flight Team on several occasions, including a few weeks ago at the MCAS Miramar Air Show in October 2010. This is the very definition of precision. Six multi-million dollar fighter jets flying in unison only a few feet from each other is an awesome sight to behold. Each pilot must be focused on the leader and their respective roles. There are six team members and six fighter jets, yet when they fly in formations they move as one team. However, this does not stop with the pilots. The maintenance and grounds crew for the Blue Angels is just as precise. I enjoy watching the pre-flight procedure as it takes place out on the flight line. Crew mechanics meticulously monitor the jets and with great precision salute their readiness to the pilots. It is only after this checkpoint occurs that the pilots taxi their way down to the runway.

This example gives a picture of what world-class performance is all about. Hours of training, consistently learning from feedback loops, team building trust, and talent selection all make for a "quality product." Imagine if your business acted in such a way? Imagine if your sales and operations divisions moved and acted as one? What if your marketing team worked side by side with manufacturing? How much better would your customer experience be?

The Gap Closure Factor for Precision is Quality (speed is a secondary GCF). When it all comes down to it, your service and/or product must be done with quality. The value your customer has placed on your services and/or products will only stay as consistent as the quality of such. The more consistent and/or better the quality, the greater the customer experience will be. McDonalds has done a great job globally of consistently building quality products for their consumers. When one goes into a McDonalds, one expects the same quality no matter what city, state or country they live in.

In Summary:

Christ exemplified compassion. How can you drive compassion with your customers without coming across as a weakness?

_____

_____

_____

_____

_____

What areas of your business do you have gaps in? Do you think your customer knows? Your Employees?

_____

_____

_____

_____

_____

What does the E910 principle mean to you?

_____

_____

_____

_____

_____

How would you define innovative customer experiences? Examples?

_____

_____

_____

_____

_____

What elements of the model does your business have improvement opportunities in?

_____

_____

_____

_____

_____

_____

How would you build the GCFs in the model? What have you seen be successful?

_____

_____

_____

_____

_____

_____

Remember the biblical principles. The relational principles are the Image, Honesty, Perception and Pay-Forward principles. The action principles are the Knowledge, E910, and Servant principles. How would you apply these to the model? Where do they fit?

_____

_____

_____

_____

_____

_____

_____

Does developing a Control Plan for your Customer Experience make sense for your organization? Why or why not?

_____

_____

_____

_____

_____

_____

Sample prayers for guidance on the Customer Experience:

Lord Jesus,

Thank you for the skills and abilities you have given me. Thank you for allowing me opportunities to grow. I ask that your will be done in my work life as I endeavor to seek and serve you in all I do. Give me knowledge that I may use wisdom and integrity when dealing with my customers. Quicken me to be proactive in bringing value to each of my clients. Grant me the opportunity to do everything I can to help them and bring a smile to their day. Give me boldness should an opportunity arise to witness for you. Keep me focused on you while bringing focus to them.

Amen.

Lord Jesus,

Thank you for the ability to learn. Thank you for your word where I can glean insights into my workplace and career. Help me to improve how I view the customer experience. Give me a chance to "be an example" in word and action to my customers. May they see integrity in me and all that I say and do. Give me the opportunity to work hard for them and treat them with the dignity I would expect myself.

Amen.

Chapter 5

Effective Team Building

Companies who effectively manage their greatest asset (the competitive advantage of great employees) will sustain great business performance long-term. Human Capital Management (HCM) is now the industry buzz-term. No matter what you call it, managing employees within an organization can make or break results. The Image Principle described in the Customer Experience chapter[21] certainly applies to employees as well. We are to treat each employee with dignity, respect and fairness as God created each one of them in His own image. This does not mean we cannot discipline employees (such as performance improvement plans or terminations) but it does mean we are to do so with as much respect as possible in all circumstances.

This chapter focuses on team development at a high level. Once we have determined to follow the Image Principle, how do we get our employees to collaborate effectively in teams? What does team mean? The modern definition of a team (Webster's On-Line) is: a number of persons associated together in work or activity: as a group on one side (as in football or a debate). Eagle Peak Leadership, a non-profit faith and workplace ministry, simply defines team as "two or more individuals working collaboratively to achieve a common goal or result." However, as most of us know, Team means so much more.

There is enormous value in teams. If a team is developed correctly, the innovation, creativity, and results stemming from that team are almost limitless. How do you view teams and team performance? Your worldview can have an impact on how you view team building. Team and team performance is about people first. Effective leadership focused on people equals world-class team performance over time. Teams can flourish even under poor leadership, but only for a short period of time. Another key tip about team development is knowledge management and learning accelerates team performance. Google, 3M, and Xerox are just three companies that are very good at managing the knowledge within their firms and ensuring teams have access to the information they need to be successful.

In 1965, Bruce Tuckman created a group development model called the forming-storming-norming-performing model. It is very popular in many corporations and is used in many learning and development organizations around the world. In this chapter we will briefly review the four steps of the model, then what the Bible states about team development. Clearly, God knows what teamwork is all about. He created the heavens and the earth and we know He is all-knowing. Being all-knowing must mean He "knows" what is best about developing teams. It is a logical conclusion. As we look at the model, be thinking about your own job and company you are employed in. Think about the teams that you are a part of (many of us serve on hundreds of teams throughout our careers). See if you can apply some learning to your team environment.

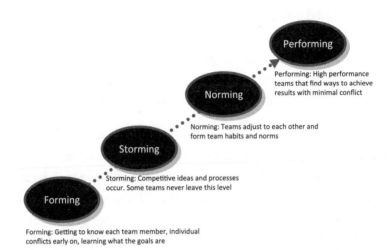

Performing: High performance teams that find ways to achieve results with minimal conflict

Norming: Teams adjust to each other and form team habits and norms

Storming: Competitive ideas and processes occur. Some teams never leave this level

Forming: Getting to know each team member, individual conflicts early on, learning what the goals are

The model (as seen in the graphic above) contains four stages of progression for a group or team. The first stage is called the Forming stage. This is where the team is first formed. Individuals are getting to know one another and are trying to learn the roles and responsibilities each member brings to the team. The team also learns what its main objectives and goals are. This stage can have early conflicts and many team members can feel uncomfortable or frustrated. It is very important to get the team focused on their vision, mission and goals. Common purpose drives better results. The Bible says where there is no vision, the people perish...[122] King Solomon recognized that without vision, it is impossible to see people get to consistent results over time. People remain lost without vision. Think about you own life for a moment. Have you ever been in the place where you have been confused about what is expected of you? Perhaps in your marriage, your education, your career? Now think carefully. In those times of confusion, how clear was the vision at the time? Let's take marriage. Marriage was designed by God, and by his design our roles in marriage interact with our spiritual roles to Him. God's vision with marriage is to teach humanity how he loves us unconditionally, how he never forsakes us, and how he wants the very best for our lives. How many Christian marriages have failed because one or both spouses have forgotten this vision and simply ignored it?

Activities you can do to help the team get through this stage effectively include vision and mission development, clear and concise goals and objectives with milestones for progress measurement along the way, icebreakers in the early meetings to enable learning about each other, immediately increase learning opportunities that will improve the individual's contribution to the team, take the team off-site to another firm or place to get out of the norm and focused, etc. you will find these activities very effective in helping the team "form."

The second stage of the model is storming. This can be a very difficult stage and research has shown that some teams never leave this level. However, if a team navigates this well, this stage can generate excitement, creativity and collaboration. Competitive ideas and processes abound in this early stage of team development. Many cross functional members begin to "stand their ground" with their specific way of doing things. I have seen teams lose weeks of momentum because they could not agree to certain project management tools to use for the team. Yet I have also seen teams move very quickly through this stage utilizing trust, confidence and an eye on the end goal.

The third stage of the model is norming. This is the level where teams begin to adjust to one another. They have taken the time to learn what each other brings to the team and have adapted where applicable to ensure the team has a common set of norms. Norms can be items such; always respond to a team member's e-mail within twenty-four hours or if you cannot get a task done on time let the team leader know as soon as possible. Teams that develop strong norms are well on their way to success. There are things to watch out for in this stage. One is "group think." A team with the Group think effect is defined as a team that consistently fosters the same opinions/decisions and begins to act as one stifling any constructive feedback or creativity. This can happen through intimidation, peer pressure, fear, risk avoidance, etc. The second item to watch for is compliance management of the norms. Some teams fail to move past this stage because they set up norms but no one really follows them. This generates low individual and team morale, enables unproductive meetings, and breaks confidence in getting results.

The fourth and last stage in the model is performing. This is where teams begin to accelerate performance and achieve results. They typically work well together yet always foster team growth and creativity. Most of the time, high performance teams are the only teams that reach this stage and sustain themselves in it even through attrition. Teams in this stage have very clear objectives, trust each other implicitly, have confidence the team can exceed goals and work hard together to achieve them. Before we understand what tips the Bible gives in association with this model, let's look at two examples of teams who have been through these stages. The first example is a personal example. I was leading an on-site services team as a first line manager and we had the opportunity to create a team that would operationalize a new quality improvement program for processes and workflows on-site where we did our work at the customer locations (national account). The forming stage for us at first was more about personality conflicts, etc. I had to get the team focused on the task at hand. We met with the Corporate team who would be supporting us on our journey to implementation. Immediately resistance began to build because the team did not believe in the vision of the program and felt it too cumbersome to really improve productivity. We battled corporate for several weeks with data analysis going back and forth on why this would or would not work. Finally, as I contemplated the next steps one day, it occurred to me to change the vision of my team, one they could believe in. I called a meeting and went on to explain that I had felt there were some parts of the program that were too cumbersome and some parts that would be very good for our business. I asked them to take on a different challenge with this. I asked them to implement the program "as is" to meet the needs of the corporate vision but along the way we as a team would document the time needed to complete each phase, the issues we had, the areas of opportunity and what we would recommend to do differently. I told them by completing the program we could then use that as leverage to improve the program. This gave them "another" purpose to focus on. They accepted the challenge.

We became the second account team to completely implement the program. The team was recognized by corporate and flown to a leadership event where they were able to share their lessons learned and how they achieved what they did. The team also documented the issues and data and we presented that to the corporate team who started looking at ways to change the program. By changing the purpose to something that all team members believed in, we were highly successful and I believe a stage four team (probably one of the best teams I have ever led).

Another great example of team development and great team work is the United States Special Forces. Whether it's the Force Recon teams of the Marine Corps, the Seals of the Navy, the Rangers of the Army, or the Special Ops Teams of the Air Force, these teams go a long way and take special care in developing their teams. Perhaps you have seen the documentaries on the Discovery or History channels. Individuals are taught to interact together in highly adverse conditions, under enormous stress to perform near impossible tasks. They need this training because their jobs require a set of skills that are extreme.

Those who are business leaders have an opportunity to learn from the special forces of the United States Military. If you can harness the energy, effort and core values of team development in the military, you can increase the effectiveness of your teams. Peter Drucker believed this. He wrote "The Army trains and develops more leaders than do all other institutions together—and with a lower casualty rate."[123] In one of the best books ever written on business leadership, authors Jason Santamaria, Vincent Martino, and Eric Clemons collaboratively explore what drives the leadership in the Marine Corps.[124] In *The Marine Corps Way; Using Maneuver Warfare to Lead a Winning Organization,* the authors show the value of applying maneuver warfare principles to leadership (additional material from this book in the leadership chapter). They speak of effective team development through disciplined processes and leaders with integrity, courage and fortitude.

As discussed earlier in this chapter, a great example from the military is the United States Navy Blue Angels Flight Squad. Made up of six multi-million dollar fighter jets, they fly in unison under enormous pressure and risk. If you have ever seen them, you know what I am talking about. I had the privilege recently of hearing one of the former pilots discuss his career and how the Blue Angels prepared as a team. He talked about purpose, planning, execution, and their foundational impact on team performance and development. Although this seems pretty straight-forward, there are many organizations that just do not get it. Though many companies try various programs and methodologies spending millions of dollars on team development, they fail to achieve high-performance effectiveness because they lack focus or intensity on the basics.

There are many examples of consistent team performance and great team development. John Wooden's unmatched college coaching of the UCLA Basketball teams where he won an unprecedented ten national championships, SWAT teams in many police departments, and corporations like Google, 3M, UPS and Apple have all shown examples of effective team performance yielding creativity and delivering consistent results.

What does the Bible say about team performance and development? As we look at the four stage team development model again, what can we learn from Scripture during each stage? Below is a model developed to visually show you how Scriptures align with the four stages. The intent is to have the reader begin to formulate thoughts about team development and how the Bible can be used to support development and improve overall performance. It is my sincere hope that readers will analyze their Bibles more and find additional Scriptures that will benefit them as they serve on or lead teams.

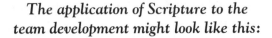

The application of Scripture to the team development might look like this:

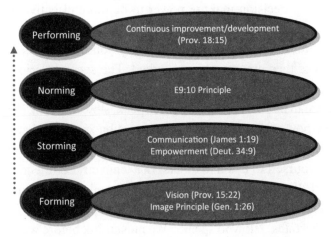

During the forming stage, team members and leaders first need to remember the Image Principle.[125] Each member of the team is made in God's image and God loves each individual. This means we should treat them with respect no matter what we agree or disagree with. Teams can have conflicts and still be respectful of each other. Another Scripture that applies to this stage is found in Proverbs.[126] King Solomon wrote, "Without counsel plans fail, but with many advisers they succeed." When you are forming a team, be sure to get the proper knowledge and coaching necessary to establish a good foundation for team development. We will be discussing choosing team members later in this chapter.

The next stage is the storming stage. There are two key Scriptures that will really help teams get through this stage effectively. The first is through empowerment. The book of Deuteronomy[127] tells the story of how Moses empowered Joshua to lead the nation of Israel. In a final act of empowerment, the Bible says that Moses laid hands on Joshua (prayed for him) and Joshua was full of the spirit of wisdom. Empowerment is a very strong, effective tool if done correctly. Empowerment does not mean blind trust. It simply means giving someone the necessary decision making power to be more effective on the job. Empowerment does not mean perfect performance either. Sometimes mistakes are made, but if one learns from the mistakes then empowerment worked. The second Scripture is found in the book of James.[128] The apostle James writes, "…let every man be swift to hear, slow to speak, slow to wrath." This is a very powerful sentence. The first portion speaks to listening. The King James Version states, "be swift to hear." Be quick or ready yourself to listen to others. In a team environment, this is crucial. We have to discipline ourselves and create norms that will enable faster and better listening among teams. The next portion states, "slow to speak." We must think before we speak. There must be care taken before making a statement. All too often we blurt out decisions, opinions or data that may not be relevant, or may be damaging to the overall team objectives. The last portion states, "slow to wrath." How many meetings or customer experiences have you had where someone reacted angrily over something they should not have? The effect is real and sometimes hurtful. We need to train ourselves to stem the tide of anger when it rises over us. Both improving communication skills and learning to empower will go a long way to fostering great team performance.

The third stage is the norming stage. As discussed in the chapter on customer experience, there is a Principle that has an overarching impact on this stage. The E910 Principle states that what ever is in your hand, do with all your might. As teams develop norms and team dynamics take shape, the more each individual strives for higher performance, the faster the overall team performs. As each team member realizes their potential and excels at what they do, they will begin to synergize with each other as part of this Principle also applies to working within teams. Whatever is in your hand means that if I am on a team, I should be giving my all for the team. If I am leading a manufacturing plant, I should be giving my all for that team. If I am on a process improvement team for the accounting department, I should be giving my very best for that team. Imagine if we all strived to do this?

The last stage is the performing stage. Proverbs 18:15 states, "the heart of the prudent getteth knowledge; and the ear of the wise seeketh knowledge." As teams begin to perform at this stage, it is very important to ensure the team is consistently improving its knowledge through best practice sharing, benchmarking and process improvement. Setting up cross-functional sessions to share knowledge can also help in keeping a team creative and innovative. Knowledge management for any team can be rewarding and improve team morale.

We have just gone through the four stage group development model and also learned what the Bible says about these stages. The Bible is filled with Scriptures that we can apply to teams and how to be a better team member.

Who is right for the team?

One of the key steps when developing teams is finding the right members for the team. Jim Collins uses the "Bus" example: getting the people in the right seat on the right bus.[129] Christ himself chose a select group for the apostleship[130] and another seventy for additional disciples (in teams of two).[131] Do you think Christ took the time to choose the right people for the right job? What if he decided that Peter was too "individually minded" when he met him? Or perhaps Matthew did not have the "proper" background to serve on the team? It is this author's belief that Jesus knew how to choose the right team members and worked to develop them during his short time prior to his death and resurrection.

There are seven key attributes to consider when choosing team members. They are (in no particular order): sense of urgency, specialized knowledge, willingness to learn, proven record for getting results, proactiveness, not afraid to take risks, and accountability. All of these attributes give teams incredible advantages in achieving results. However, there is an eighth underlying attribute as well. That attribute is integrity. Integrity must be the foundation for all other attributes.

Let's briefly look at the seven other attributes. Having a sense of urgency means that you know how to balance development and execution, discussion and action, and risk and reward. Teams (and individuals) must understand that having a sense of urgency can be a tremendous strength. All too often teams fail because they failed to see the "urgency" needed for a situation or objective. As noted in the leadership chapters, President Abraham Lincoln once stated, "Things may come to those who wait, but only things left by those who hustle."

In the book of Revelation,[132] Jesus himself warned the Laodiciean church of complacency in their ministry. Instead of being "urgent" about their activities and results, they became complacent. Team members also need specialized knowledge. This goes without saying. Every team has objectives. In order to meet these objectives, a certain set of criteria or knowledge must be prevalent in the team. A process improvement team focused on improving employment application defect errors better have some knowledge of how the human resources process works. The third attribute is having a willingness to learn. There are many employees that for whatever reason do not continue to develop themselves or to learn. I have seen many of my peers, management and others settle into a position and resolve to stay or expect to grow without doing more on their own. Identifying potential team members that have a desire for continuous development will enable stronger team collaboration as this attribute will naturally play out in a team environment in most cases.

The next attribute is a proven record for delivering results. Let's face it. We need teams who can deliver results—on time. When choosing potential individuals to participate in teams, look for the individuals who have proven they can deliver results. This will become a driving force within the team if coached well. Teams also need proactiveness and the willingness to take risks. These two attributes go hand in hand. Individuals who are proactive and that take risks will create energy in a team environment. Typically, a team with these attributes as a norm will drive *better* results as they will not be afraid to crash and burn within the process. In doing so, creativity flourishes and improvements are made. The last attribute is accountability. Teams need individuals who are accountable to their commitments, actions and their mistakes. This builds team synergy over time and team members learn to trust a little deeper and confidence in each other grows.

In Summary:

Reflect on a time when you were on a team that struggled. What were some of the reasons for that struggle? How did you feel as a team member?

_____

_____

_____

_____

_____

Why do some teams never get past the Storming stage?

_____

_____

_____

_____

_____

_____

_____

When the Bible talks about us being made in the image of God, why is this hard to apply to our peers in business?

_____

_____

_____

_____

_____

On the last team you served on, what stage would you say the team achieved?

_____

_____

_____

_____

_____

Read James 1:19. What does this biblical verse mean to you? Which of the three commands do you struggle with?

_____

_____

_____

_____

_____

When you think about high performance teams (like the Blue Angels), what comes to mind?

_____

_____

_____

_____

_____

The Bible is clear on how we are to perform our work. What can you do in the next thirty days to improve your performance at work?

_____

_____

_____

_____

_____

Sample prayer for guidance on Team Development:

> *Lord Jesus,*
>
> *Thank you for your wisdom and blessings in my life. Help me to be a better team member in the workplace. Give me strength and knowledge to improve my performance and use this as an opportunity for me to witness for your glory. Let me see my peers, my management and my customers the way you see them. Help me to lead teams more effectively and choose the right people for the right job. Most of all, open my ears to your word and use me for your kingdom in the present job you have given me.*
>
> *Amen.*

Chapter 6

Does the Bible Really Talk About Strategy?

In the movie *The Patriot,* Mel Gibson plays the part of Benjamin Martin, a farmer in South Carolina in 1776. A French and Indian War veteran with a savage past, Benjamin decides to stay out of the Revolution against Great Britain mainly due to guilt on actions in the earlier war. His two eldest sons disagree with his view and one immediately enlists in the militia. Later, as the eldest son is being arrested for treason against the crown, the second eldest son is shot by the British soldier, Lord Tavington, a ruthless man. This all takes place in front of Benjamin Martin and his entire family. This act of murder and arrest leads Martin to join the war and become one of its heroes. During the last battle scene, a strategy is put forth by Benjamin Martin. He proposes using militia to fill the front lines and engage initially with the Redcoats. After firing two shots, the militia were to retreat back over a hill where Continental Army regulars would be waiting. The strategy worked. Martin had assumed the Redcoats would see the militia front lines as weak (they had "run" in previous battles) and this time the British would want to follow and "crush the rebellion." They did and the Continental Army came away with a significant victory.

Like Benjamin Martin, we all inter-relate with strategy throughout our lives. Strategy plays a pivotal role in much of life. Men and women have strategies to find the right person to date. What to say, where to go, etc. Sports teams use strategy in game situations shifting execution as they need to. The University of Texas football team had to switch offensive strategies in the 2010 College Football National Championship game due to unforeseen injury and still played a very good game. Parents have strategies for raising their kids. Parents pick certain schools, sports, arts participation, and other activities in hopes of the best development for their children.

Of course, it's no different in the marketplace. Strategies take place at all levels of any organization and every job has a strategic intent. This is consistent throughout the global marketplace. The strategic intent for the mail associate position with the company, MITIE (in the UK), is to provide daily mail service on-site for a customer with expertise and efficiency. UK (and other European countries) customers partner with MITIE and other outsource providers with the strategic intent of improving productivity while lowering operational costs. Strategy is the foundation for these decisions. Whether you are a police officer, contractor, receptionist, accountant or restaurant manager, your position has strategic value and is part of a broader strategy. These examples are not exclusive as all of us are involved in strategy in some way or another in the workplace. Since this is the case, shouldn't we be looking for ways to expand ourselves in how to develop sound and strong strategy then also how to execute flawlessly? Understanding how to develop and execute a better strategy for your position and its integration with the organizational strategy will enable you to be more successful in your current role and provide opportunity for you to make an impact in the workplace.

According to Webster's dictionary, strategy is defined as "a plan, method, or series of maneuvers or stratagems for obtaining a specific goal or result."[133] Another definition is "the science or art of combining and employing the means of war in planning and directing large military movements and operations." Strategy is a comprehensive set of activities and actions intended to produce specific results. It is important to define what strategy is. The reason is that many do not fully comprehend the true definition and only focus on parts of the definition. For example, I have witnessed some executive teams that focused on the "activities around developing a strategy" while failing to understand how the strategy will get the results (execution). I have also seen organizations spend very little time in developing the right strategy and even when they executed flawlessly, they still failed. Individually and corporately, we must fully be aware of the "whole" strategy, from development to planning to execution, in order to achieve success.

We can see this through examples around the world. There are many examples of failures and successes in strategy. In the United States, Coca-Cola is famous for its failed strategy of launching "New Coke" (though Coca-Cola is still an excellent company when one measures against *A*-Model leadership). New Coke never really did take off and the company had to abandon the strategy at a huge cost. Positively, UPS has done a great job developing and executing on its marketing strategy. Their marketing and advertising has done a wonderful job of creating the message that UPS knows global supply chain management. For several years, we have all seen or heard the line, *What can Brown do for you?* The marketing campaign/strategy was considered very successful. Accenture did a great job of shifting marketing strategies when their primary endorsee, Tiger Woods, fell into a major personal crisis caused by his poor judgment and sin. Accenture made the decision to stop advertising using Tiger Woods as its central theme and immediately replaced Tiger in their marketing campaign with a series of advertisements using animals. One advertisement I saw in Chicago, has four bullfrogs and one bullfrog is leaping over three other bullfrogs. The sign stated, "Play Quantum Leap Frog." While I have not seen the formal results, I would venture to say that Accenture's return on investment did not see a negative impact. Other examples of good strategies are Southwest Airlines (point to point regional service), Starbucks Coffee (sell the value of the experience of coffee), Apple (developing new markets, itunes, iPOD, Ipad, etc.), and Corner Bakery (customer experience focus). Globally, there are examples as well. HSBC has done a great job with its strategy of selling values in the Banking industry. Through great advertising on many jet-ways around the world, they show that many people view things differently based on their values. We all value things differently. HSBC has built a strategy to sell itself as a bank and financial institution that understands values. In fact, their former Chairman, Stephen Green, wrote a very good business finance book called *Good Value,* where he explains his thoughts on money, economies and good business.

So what can we learn from these examples? Is there a simpler way to get better at developing and executing strategy? As we have stated, developing strategy is a very critical skill, but just as critical is the execution of the strategy. Knowing where you are going is meaningless unless you know how you are getting there. Once you have developed the how, it is equally important to execute. As leaders, we must develop ourselves in understanding, creating, and executing strategies. The objective of this chapter is to get you thinking about the value of understanding strategy and give you a simple model to use built on biblical principles. I highly recommend you look into other sources such as *Harvard Business Review,* London Business School and National University of Singapore. There are excellent books as well like *Blue Ocean Strategy* and *Executing Your Strategy.* The key is to take the time to review and learn. It's an investment that will pay dividends for life.

The Bible has plenty to say about strategy as well and there are many examples of strategy given in Scripture. Since God is the only omniscient, omnipresent, and omnipotent being, it is a valid conclusion that he is the inventor of strategy. If he is the inventor of strategy, then we should pay attention to what his word tells us about it. Grab your Bibles and let's look at two examples of God-given strategy to two different men in the Bible and see what we can learn. The first example is found in the book of Joshua. Joshua was the successor to Moses and had just led the nation of Israel across the Jordan River into the land promised to them by God. Joshua was a faithful leader and humble servant to God. We pick up the story at the end of chapter five. Joshua was standing by Jericho (an enemy city) when he caught sight of a man facing him with his sword drawn. Joshua went to him and asked, are you for us or for our adversaries? The reply from the stranger was powerful. He said, "Nay, but as Captain of the host of the Lord am I now come."[134] Joshua then fell on his face in worship. He also asks, "what saith my Lord to his servant?" The Captain replied loose your shoes from your feet for where you are standing is holy. Joshua did so.[135]

Before we continue with the story and strategy for the destruction of Jericho, there are important tips in these Scriptures for us to learn as Christians. The first learning is that Joshua, who was confident in his relationship and strength in God, went to the stranger to ask who are you for? Joshua did not let fear disable his ability to move forward. The reason is that he firmly believed God was in complete control of his life. We can learn to allow God complete access to our lives and to give us strength to face any fears that come our way. The second learning is that as Christ (many scholars and theologians believe this visit was from the pre-incarnate Christ for many reasons)[136] stated he was Captain of the hosts of the Lord Joshua bowed down to worship. We can learn that as we recognize Christ in every area of our life, we should immediately worship him for who he is. Worship goes a long way to preparing Christians for greater use in the workplace. The third learning from this passage of Scripture is that Joshua asked the Lord what he would say to his servant. Joshua did not start out with telling Christ how he has been wronged by others or his sins, fears, etc. Joshua asked, what did you want to say to me Lord? We must learn to listen to our Lord as well. We must want to hear from him. As we discussed in the spiritual disciplines chapter, solitude, reading God's Word and prayer are all great ways to listen to the voice of the Lord.

The story continues in chapter six where Christ gives Joshua explicit instructions on how to deal with the city of Jericho. This city was impenetrable at the time of Joshua and it brought fear into the hearts of the nation of Israel. These instructions were a little different to say the least. The strategy given by God was to have the nation of Israel march around the city of Jericho once a day for six days. Soldiers, Priests, The Ark of the Covenant and others were to make the trip and everyone was supposed to keep strictly silent in doing so. On the seventh day, they were to walk around the city of Jericho for seven times. On the seventh time, Joshua was to shout to the people to make noise as the trumpets blew. This was the first time they were to make any noise in seven days and it was to be deafening. Joshua took these instructions from the Captain of the hosts of the Lord and passed them on to the people of Israel. The people executed the strategy perfectly. The walls of Jericho fell on that seventh day as did the enemies within. Now you may be asking what does this have to do with strategy in the workplace? I believe we can learn several principles from this story that will help us with the many strategies we participate in, including those at work.

The first principle we can learn is that as Christians we need to be in tune with God to truly allow ourselves to become better at developing and executing strategies. Just as Joshua was focused on his relationship with God, so should we be. Joshua was prepared to hear from the Lord. Are you prepared to hear from God about your work life? Do you invite the Lord to be a part of your daily decisions on the job? Have you asked God for wisdom, counsel and direction on strategic areas for your company, division, department or position? Being in tune with God means we understand his song (commands) and desire to play the notes (living holy before him) of the musical composition he has created for each of our lives. Blaise Pascal once stated, "the serene beauty of a holy life is the most powerful influence in the world next to the power of God."[137] This influence can help prepare you for strategy development and execution.

The second principle we can learn is that there is clear linkage with vision/purpose to strategy. The strategy outlined by the Captain was in line with God's vision for Israel inhabiting the Promised Land. What is the vision your strategy is tied to? Do you understand the vision completely? The vision for any organization (or position) must be clear and provide purpose. Purpose in work is fast becoming critically important globally, especially as generation Y or the millennial generation moves into worker ranks. Studies have shown that the younger generations look for deeper purpose in their work. In his book, *Common Purpose*, Joel Kurtzman describes the common purpose of Carnival Cruise Lines, the world's largest cruise ship operator. Carnival's common purpose is to create an experience for its customers that they will remember forever. Everything at Carnival must align with this common purpose.[138] When developing strategies and executing them, employees must feel there is a purpose behind the strategy to truly be effective. The nation of Israel saw the purpose in the strategy communicated by Joshua. They believed in it and set out to achieve results. They had common purpose.

The third principle we can learn is Joshua clearly communicated the strategy to the nation of Israel. Once the strategy was developed, there was clear communication of it. Joshua did not elaborate, take away or add anything else. He kept the communication concise and clear. Often times, companies fail in communicating their strategies. Complexity replaces clarity, mixed messages contaminate strategic purpose and so on. I have seen in many companies where the strategic vision is set forth as profitable revenue growth. While this is certainly a good purpose, I have seen actions within several divisions of the same companies contradict the overall purpose. For example, sales representatives in one company were being compensated on revenue signings without significant emphasis on profits. This created a large number of deals with very low margins which contradicted the profitable revenue growth vision. As mentioned in the leadership chapter of this book, communication skills are critical, even more so when discussing strategy.

The fourth principle we can learn is that Joshua and his leaders ensured the people executed on-time and met objectives (like remaining quiet for seven days). Remember the definition of strategy from earlier in this chapter? According to Webster's dictionary, strategy is defined as "a plan, method, or series of maneuvers or stratagems for obtaining a specific goal or result." Good strategies get results. Authors Mark Morgan, Raymond Levitt and William Malek in their excellent book, *Executing Your Strategy; How to break it down and get it done*, open their book with, "The global business landscape is littered with expensive, well-intended strategies that failed in the execution phase." They go on to state that "studies have found that less than ten percent of effectively formulated strategies carry through to successful implementation."[139] Poor communication, poor quality, and ineffective processes are just some of the reasons for failure. As Christians, God expects us to perform at our best in whatever we are doing.[140] This includes executing strategy.

How do we develop and execute great strategies? More important, how do we use the biblical principles just discussed and apply them to strategic planning and execution? The *Define-Differentiate-Develop-Deliver* or Quad-D Model is a simple process to follow when creating, developing and executing strategy. You can use this process when thinking about your current position, your organization or your future career goals. The first step in the model is Define. This step must first start with a careful analysis of your organization's vision (with input from others—a strategy team). As we learned earlier, strong vision and common purpose are essential to successful strategic results. As an organization defines its strategy, it must understand where it is headed at all levels, in all jobs. Deutsche Post DHL, a global shipping and supply chain logistics company, defined its vision centered on global logistics. Instead of focusing on just one region, Deutsche Post DHL focuses on a global supply chain as its core business. The company's website boasts, "Today, DHL's international network links more than 220 countries and territories worldwide. DHL also offers unparalleled expertise in express, air and ocean freight, overland transport, contract logistics solutions as well as international mail services."[141] With a clear vision on global logistics, the overall company group (including DHL) generated revenues of forty-six billion euros in 2009. There are many ways to define your strategy. Once your vision is solidified, strategy can be built around it through competitive analysis, market trends, market intelligence and organizational innovation. Michael Porter writes of key elements of strategy, and these elements are a good place to start. There are five key elements when defining your strategy. Customers, suppliers, socio-political-geo factors, financial drivers and competition are the elements to consider. Who are your customers? What social, political or geographical factors must you consider? What financial drivers will your organization use? Revenue growth, profit growth, low margins, high margins, etc. Also, who are your competitors and what are they currently doing in the industry? These are all very important questions to answer when defining your strategy.

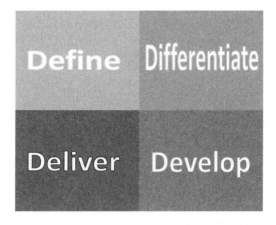

The second step is to differentiate your strategy. In one of the best books ever written on strategy, authors W. Chan Kim and Renee Mauborgne explain how to create uncontested market space through what they termed as *Blue Ocean Strategy*.[142] The premise of the book is that most companies focus on competitive based "red ocean" strategies where there are boundaries, limited market capacity and profits. The authors propose that in order for a company to keep sustainable profits consistently over time, that company must create a "blue ocean" strategy. Blue ocean strategies make the competition irrelevant because the "blue ocean" is new market space with unlimited resources and better profits. One of the early examples given in the book is with Cirque du Soleil, the Canada based circus company. By creating a "blue ocean" for circus strategy, Cirque du Soleil achieved the same revenue levels in less than twenty years that it took circus giants Ringling Bros. and Barnum Bailey more than one hundred years to attain.[143] How? Cirque du Soleil focused on a new strategy that created a new market space. Cirque du Soleil focused on a strategy that catered to adults, emphasizing themes by show, using artistry and music more and staying away from animal shows and traditional circus acts. Since no one else was doing this, Cirque du Soleil reaped the profits and made the competition irrelevant.

There are several tools described in *Blue Ocean Strategy* that are very helpful in differentiating your strategy. These tools include the strategy canvas, the four actions framework, and the Eliminate-Reduce-Raise-Create grid.[144]

The third step in the Quad D Strategy Model is Develop. By now, you have defined a good strategy in line with your company's vision and purpose. You have also differentiated your strategy from that of your competition and have looked at ways to create new markets. Now it's time to fully develop the strategy. This step involves the basics of business. Answering questions like how will you go to market with your strategy, how will you fund the strategy, and how will you communicate the strategy and gain employee and shareholder (if applicable) buyin? What does the execution plan look like? Have your customers tested the strategy or at the very least provided input? Nilofer Merchant,[145] CEO of Rubicon Consulting, states there are five structural elements for strategy she believes will deliver world class execution. These five structural elements are briefly described as pulled from an article off the Entrepreneur website. "Element 1 is Power Distribution. Power distribution dictates who's involved, how much information each individual can access, and the decision-making process. Make sure that the inner working of the group matches the culture and values of the parent organization. If your company is as free-flowing as Google, don't bind people with conservative rules that eliminate communal sharing of ideas or the development innovative solutions. Element 2 is Decision Making. The way that decisions are made in organizations determines how ideas are generated and which ideas are considered. The way decisions are made influences how these ideas are carried out later. Does decision making in your organization flow top-down or bottom-up? Who are the holders of the power to decide which ideas advance and which are eliminated? If ideas are valued in your culture, there's a strong likelihood that it might not matter who generates the ideas.

"Element 3 is Idea Generation. How ideas are generated affects the quantity and quality of these ideas, which directly affects the number of viable strategy options. A company that has an annual strategy meeting with a brainstorming component that encompasses input from many directions within the company uses one type of idea generation. The Google model involves having employees use 20 percent of their time for innovation. They test and grow projects. Some projects are nurtured and provide the company with revenue. Others are killed off. It's even possible that original projects may mutate into something different. Element 4 is Process. Process is the way that ideas are handled and consumed within organizations. Process defines the way that agreements and commitments are made and managed, and how well people understand what is happening and what to do. The process-driven organization avoids wasting employee time and energy. People in this type of company reach agreement that an action is valuable, develop a process around it, and set it in motion. Process may be communicated to a team in writing, by word of mouth or in other ways. Agreement is critical to the understanding of process within an organization. Element 5 is People. In an organization of any size, people bring their domain knowledge, talents, and perspectives to strategy creation. Often people are viewed as the first point of strategy failure, but they are actually the last point of failure in a long series of cascading interactions. Put another way, very bright, creative, motivated people can fail if they are embedded in a strategy creation structure process where power, decision making, idea generation, or process are broken. Each of the five elements is critical to the strength, balance, and practicality of the proposed strategy. Tighten up around these five and watch your team's next strategy succeed beyond your plans."[146] Mrs. Merchant has it right. These elements, when done correctly, will solidify your strategy and improve its overall performance.

The last step in the Quad D Strategy Model is Deliver. I cannot emphasize this enough. Companies can be fantastic at developing a great strategy only to fail in its execution. Organizations should spend equal intensity on both developing and executing strategies. One of the first factors an organization should look at is the current culture of the company. The first time I heard the statement "culture eats strategy for lunch" was sitting in a customer's conference room in Charlotte, NC. This Senior Vice President was trying to tell my team that we needed to better understand the culture of the company and develop plans to help integrate the culture with the new strategy we were proposing or we would fail. In the same meeting he went on to share that he felt our company had a sense of arrogance at times which is dangerous for strategic execution. He was correct.

When executing a strategy, we need to consider change management, communication, and measuring for results. Change management includes cultural and behavioral change management and how organizations deal with strategic change. Effective change management plans alleviate tension and promote value of the change. Organizations should spend time developing the value message of the change tied to the vision and purpose of the organization. When employees, shareholders, suppliers and customers see the linkage to the vision and mission of the company, it builds trust and confidence in the strategy. There are four steps in delivering (executing) a great strategy. The first step is to develop an execution plan. King Solomon wrote "without counsel plans fail, but with many advisers they succeed."[147] Another verse tells us "plans are established by counsel..."[148] When developing the execution plan, gather feedback from select employees, suppliers and customers and ensure the feedback covers all functional areas of the business. Incorporate this feedback into the execution plan. In doing so, others will feel they had a part in the overall strategic implementation of the company.

The second step is to establish a measurement plan. There should be metrics tied to every milestone defined in the strategy. The idea is not analysis paralysis, but there should be a performance dashboard created so results can be monitored and tweaks made if needed. All too often companies wait too long in understanding strategic results and suffer losses because of it. Its is a careful balance however, because some strategies will take time to develop and with the short term philosophy of the DJIA, FTSE, or other global markets, some companies act too quickly or avoid long-term strategic planning all together. The balance must be kept straight through critical metrics analysis. How will you know your strategy is effective in sixty days, six months, sixteen months, sixty months? Winston Churchill once remarked, "However beautiful the strategy, you should occasionally look at the results."

The third step in delivering on a great strategy is establishing results oriented performance goals. Every job in the company should have performance goals in line with the vision and strategy of the company. This drives ability in understanding positional value of each job in relation to the organization's vision and it gives the employee clear objectives for his or her position. Xerox uses the performance excellence plan (PEP) model where every job has an annual PEP tied to the company's goals, values and strategy. It starts each year with the CEO's PEP (Ursula Burns) and each PEP developed at every level of the organization relates. Typically, the lower the levels into the company, the more tactical and granular the performance targets get. Establishing these targets at every level will ensure the organization is focused on the same objectives.

The last step in delivering on a great strategy is to invest in your people. Hundreds of business books, business schools and university studies have shown the value in investing in employees through reward and recognition, education, and other benefits. Employees who are highly motivated, loyal, skilled and confident will attain higher performance, period. This is not rocket science and applies to every area of the world. Last year, I spent time with a team on-site at a global customer's location in Beijing. This team was highly motivated and confident. They were confident in their management and in their performance. The customer gave me feedback that day that he was very appreciative of our team. I saw firsthand the effectiveness of a highly motivated, confident team. In Mumbai, this was not the case for our global team. The on-site team in Mumbai was not confident in management and certainly was not motivated or recognized the way they should have been. The result was customer dissatisfaction and operational issues that needed to be dealt with.

Spending time understanding strategic importance is time well spent. As you consider the principles learned from the Bible, business examples and the Quad-D Strategy model, the most important thing to remember is to continue to learn both how to develop and execute strategy and balance your learning in both. Sun Tzu wrote, "Strategy without tactics is the slowest route to victory. Tactics without strategy is the noise before defeat."

In Summary:

Why is strategy difficult for many leaders?

_____

_____

_____

_____

_____

_____

_____

Why do good strategies fail?

_____

_____

_____

_____

_____

_____

_____

What did you learn about strategy from the example given on the story of Joshua?

_____

_____

_____

_____

_____

Reflect on the Quad-D Strategy Model. Which step do you find difficult and why?

_____

_____

_____

_____

_____

Spend time reflecting on your current job. How does it relate to the strategy of the organization?

_____

_____

_____

_____

_____

List examples of companies with great strategies that you have interacted with either as a customer, employee or supplier. Why were their strategies great?

_____

_____

_____

_____

_____

Sample prayer for guidance on Strategy:

> *Lord Jesus, I am humbled by your Word. I am grateful for the ability to learn. Thank you for your wisdom and knowledge. Help me to be better at developing and executing strategies. Teach me to listen to others when developing strategies. Open my mind to alternatives and help me to be creative. Most important, keep me in your will as I endeavor to learn more on this topic.*
>
> *Amen.*

Chapter 7

Continuous Improvement Starts with God

Several years ago, I led a Lean Six Sigma "Black Belt" project at a global bank. Lean Six Sigma is the combination of two different improvement methodologies (Lean Thinking and Six Sigma) and both are very good. Lean Thinking focuses on the reduction of waste (waste defined as motion, transportation, inventory, defects, etc.) with the goal of improving the velocity of a process (faster through-put). One of the key tools of Lean Thinking is value stream mapping. This tool visually shows the value stream of a process including all inputs and outputs and identifies bottlenecks. Six Sigma focuses on reducing variation in a process with the goal of reducing defects. One of the key measures of Six Sigma is DPMO or defects per million opportunities which simply means for every million widgets (or invoices, helpdesk calls, or any other product or service result) there would only be 3.4 defects at "six sigma"—a mathematical result achieving significantly reduced variation. The healthcare and airline industries typically have many processes running at six sigma.

This particular project took over four months to complete and focused on improving process cycle time and the reduction of waste including defects for a particular operational process. As I led this project, I couldn't help but notice the variation in the team's personalities related to continuous improvement. Some members of the team were perfectly willing to maintain status quo for the operational process we were trying to improve. Their feedback was we are meeting standards now, so why change things? Other members of the team were excited about the possibility of improving the current process. So why the difference? It is not just with this project but really it's with any area of life. Continuous improvement means different things to many people.

In Japan, the term is Kaizen. Kaizen means "continuous improvement" and the Japanese have done an outstanding job integrating this philosophy into their workplaces. The Toyota Production System is a wonderful example of a practical improvement program for an organization and has been customized for many different industries under the Lean Manufacturing umbrella. I have visited several companies in Tokyo and have been impressed by the focus on quality. However, I have also been to India, Brazil and a number of other places that while they exceed operational performance targets in many cases, they still have a very different culture when it comes to continuous improvement. My goal is not to judge these different views but to offer up an objective viewpoint as found in the Bible.

What is important to learn as a Christian is that God expects us to continually improve in our lives. He wants us to have deeper relationships, perform better on the job, and most important, He wants us to continue to grow (improve) in our relationship with Him. Now let's focus on practical business methodologies we can apply to our jobs and organizations as well as biblical principles for continuous improvement.

The need for continuous improvement is global and many industries are now integrating improvement methodologies and tools as part of the "everyday norm" for business. Throughout history, mankind has evolved (continuously improved) our livelihoods and our cultures. At the macro level, we have seen huge changes over thousands of years in large part, driven by needs and wants, through continuous improvement activities. Examples are endless and those in the modern age include the Panama Canal, the Chunnel (the train tunnel under the English Channel), the world-wide web, video-streaming, cellular technology, and air/space travel.

As we take a look at the micro-levels (day-to-day activities) of improvement, we can see how these macro-level improvements have increased productivity and efficiencies in our lives. I don't remember what I did twenty years ago when I went to the grocery store without a cell phone. How many trips back to the store would have been eliminated had I been able to place the call while standing in the aisle? Too many to count. Today, my wife can contact me with any additional request or I can call home for clarification on a product or brand from any grocery store I visit. Another example is Skype. "Skypeing" has become synonymous with video-streaming. People all over the world can speak to loved ones and friends over the internet and see them through video on the screen at the same time. All of this at no cost. Yet another example of continuous improvement and constant innovation is Apple. Through their iPod technology, we now have the ability to play thousands of songs off of one device and customize playlists according to our favorites. These three examples have "improved" the quality of life for millions of people. More important, look at healthcare and other industries where immediate physical impact to lives can be seen in continuous improvements. In fact, in the U.S. healthcare industry, Lean Thinking has become a critical part of many of the top healthcare organizations in the world, including Boston's John Hopkins Hospital, The Cleveland Clinic and the UCLA Medical Center. The ability to perform accurate surgeries has dramatically improved and stays in hospital rooms have significantly declined year after year due to focus on continuous healthcare improvement.

So how do we develop in continuous improvement? What steps can each of us take to get started with continuous improvement? There are two specific methodologies I will describe for application in our jobs and organizations. One comes from Lean Thinking and the other comes from Six Sigma. Both give you a framework or set of steps to perform continuous improvement actions. Further development is needed to truly understand and master these methodologies. Hopefully, after this chapter, you will want to develop more in this area and there are many resources to help you. The first methodology or tool is called 5S or *sort, set-in-order, shine, standardize and sustain* (sometimes there is a sixth "S" added for "safety"). The Japanese perfected this methodology and it comes from Lean Manufacturing. Many corporations have changed the "S's" over time to reflect their vision of it. In fact, these five words are a variation, but one I found very helpful and effective to remember.

5S is a very simple process; however, its effectiveness is proven. 5S delivers a clean, organized, standard process and work environment and maintains these results through sustainable controls and management. As a working example, we will use "ABC Company" and look at their accounting department. Let's assume the executive leadership of ABC Co. has asked that 5S be used as a pilot in the accounting department. *Sort* is the first step or phase in the 5S process. During the *sort* phase, the work or process environment is analyzed for potential improvements. The accounting manager would first review all workspaces including desks, file cabinets, aisles, and conference rooms for unnecessary items such as furniture, equipment, old files, waste, etc. These items would be identified for removal with a plan to where it will be removed to (garbage, storage, donation, or other). During this phase, the purpose of *sort* is to identify actions that need to be taken to begin improvements. There are tools such as Red Tag and simple list management that enable successful sorting. The second step or phase in 5S is *set-in-order.* During this phase, the accounting manager would begin to organize for effectiveness keeping the department's processes in mind for highest productivity capability. This would include improved layouts of workspaces, labeling, removal of items identified during the *sort* phase, and process workflow improvement. The third 5S step or phase is *shine.* During the *shine* phase, the manager would conduct thorough cleaning in all areas. Once the cleaning or housekeeping is done, a housekeeping checklist and process is developed to ensure the areas stay cleaned.

The fourth step or phase is *standardize.* During this phase, the manager would develop best practices through benchmarking to standardize certain processes or tools. Perhaps, the manager develops a time management system and has all of the team trained and using the new system. This is just one example of hundreds that can be developed during this phase. Another critical action during this phase is the development of standard operating procedures. This is to ensure everyone is performing the same tasks to produce the same results effectively. The last phase in 5S is the *sustain* phase. During this phase, a control plan including a 5S checklist is developed to sustain the improvements that 5S has brought to the accounting department. The manager needs to measure progress on a consistent basis. Metrics such as training completion, cleanliness results, use of standard operating procedures, and overall compliance will tell the manager a message. The message may state the team needs more training or perhaps processes need tweaking. The message may be very positive and the team is in full compliance and results show it. In either case, without measurement, the manager truly cannot know the variation or scope of the results over a period of time. As stated earlier, this is a brief overview of 5S. I would highly recommend that you search and find resources available to further develop your knowledge and skill with this methodology and toolset.[149] Organizations like the Lean Enterprise Institute, Lean Thinking Network, and Infor are valuable sources for learning more about 5S and Lean Thinking and Manufacturing.

The second methodology we can all learn a great deal from comes from the Six Sigma world. One of the best concise definitions is from iSixSigma. This organization defines six sigma as *"Six Sigma at many organizations simply means a measure of quality that strives for near perfection. But the statistical implications of a Six Sigma program go well beyond the qualitative eradication of customer-perceptible defects. It's a methodology that is well rooted in mathematics and statistics. The objective of Six Sigma Quality is to reduce process output variation so that on a long term basis, which is the customer's aggregate experience with our process over time, this will result in no more than 3.4 defect Parts Per Million (PPM) opportunities (or 3.4 Defects Per Million Opportunities—DPMO). For a process with only one specification limit (Upper or Lower), this results in six process standard deviations between the mean of the process and the customer's specification limit (hence, 6 Sigma). For a process with two specification limits (Upper and Lower), this translates to slightly more than six process standard deviations between the mean and each specification limit such that the total defect rate corresponds to equivalent of six process standard deviations."*[150] The definition is a good foundation for the methodology we are going to briefly overview. If you understand the rigor behind six sigma, then you should trust the toolsets being used to achieve these types of results.

DMAIC methodology is an acronym that stands for *Define-Measure-Analyze-Improve-Control*. This is a five phase methodology typically used for improving variation (reducing defects) in any given process. The intent here is not to conduct a deep dive into each of these areas (there are literally hundreds of tools and processes to consider). The intent of bringing DMAIC for your learning is to enable a *systems thinking* approach for your everyday problems at work. Let's revisit ABC Company and their accounting department. Let's assume the VP for Accounting wants to use DMAIC as a way of reducing rework in the Accounts Receivables department. The Accounts Receivables department has been having trouble meeting a fifteen day invoice generation target. Using DMAIC as a way of thinking, the process would look something like this. You would start with *Define.* During this phase, you would identify the problem statement, the goal statement, team members and stakeholders who could help resolve, risks to the process and develop a hi-level process map of the current invoice generation process. Tools typically used during the Define phase include the project charter, stakeholders analysis, SIPOC (hi-level process map) and risks management. Once you have completed these activities, the team would look to *Measure* the current process. During the measure phase, the team would further define the invoice generation process through detailed process mapping. An easy way to achieve this is to have the team jot down process steps onto post-it notes (one step per note page) individually then collectively place the notes on a board or wall. At this point there will be some confusion and most likely variation in the process itself. Next, you have the team collaboratively work through defining the current state process and come to an agreement on it.

Other tools typically used during the Measure phase besides a variety of process mapping tools are spaghetti diagrams (layout-workflow mapping), data collection plans, data analysis of current state data, and a detailed risks analysis. The Accounts Receivable team would put together a data collection plan where they will measure all key steps of their invoice generation process. They would also develop detailed process steps including decision points and sub-processes. Once these activities are complete, the team then has a firm grasp on the current state process and has captured initial data from it. During the *Analyze* phase, the team would analyze the data and process to determine defects, root causals, and test for statistical significance if applicable. Tools used during the Analyze phase include 5-Whys, Fishbone diagram, Hypothesis testing, Value Add Analysis, and data mining. ABC Company's accounting team has now identified root causes for their invoice generation process and has brainstormed improvements for these root causals.

The next phase in DMAIC is the *Improve* phase. Many people find this phase to be the "fun" phase because idea generation and solution validation can be fun to develop. During this phase, teams brainstorm solutions and then further develop those solutions. Once solutions have been developed, they are piloted to measure for improvement. New process maps are created that incorporate the changes/improvements and training is performed so that all employees understand the improved process. Tools used during the Improve phase include a variety of brainstorming tools, Pugh Matrix, process mapping, training materials and data analysis of pilot results. Getting back to the ABC Co., the team has now come up with proven solutions to improve their invoice generation cycle time and have begun training their team members on the new improvements.

The improvements are now in place but that does not guarantee sustainable results. Human nature sometimes draws teams back into old habits. Unforeseen factors may impact the results in ninety days. So how do we mitigate all of this? This is the purpose of the *Control* phase. During this phase, the team develops metrics, control plans, risk mitigation plans, and escalation plans to ensure sustainable results. A control plan enables the management team to consistently measure for performance and understand the next steps should variation occur. Tools used during this phase include control plans, FMEAs, escalation processes, and simple checklists. Back to our example, the Accounts Receivables department has now improved their invoice generation process and has set new targets. They are monitoring them via a control plan and team members have been recognized for an outstanding achievement.

Winston Churchill once stated, "Continuous efforts, not strength or intelligence, is the key to unlocking our potential."[151] These efforts combined with a continuous improvement mindset are virtually unstoppable. Both the 5S and DMAIC methodologies were explored to allow you to better understand how to develop continuous improvement habits and drive results in doing so. You may be asking by now, so what does the Bible have to do with continuous improvement? I believe the Bible has plenty to share and we will look at several principles inside of its pages.

The Word of God and Continuous Improvement

In the Pentateuch (first five books of the Bible), there is a great story tucked away in the book of Exodus.[152] Moses and the nation of Israel had just come out of Egypt where they had been oppressed for years. God had chosen Moses to be the leader to take them to the Promised Land. Moses' father-in-law, Jethro, had heard about all of the great things God was doing and paid a visit to Moses. Moses begins to share the great things God did and Jethro celebrates in worship and praise to the Lord alongside his son-in-law. The next day,[153] we are told that Moses goes about his daily work and sits as a judge (think of the American court system today) ruling on the disagreements and disputes of the entire nation. This work is exhausting and time consuming as Moses judges from morning until evening. Jethro observes this and asks Moses, why do you sit alone and what is this you are doing for the people? Moses replies and states that he is the judge and must decide on disputes among the people using God's laws as the framework. Jethro responds and makes a profound yet simple statement and says what you are doing is not good.[154] Jethro goes on to tell Moses that he should establish a system of delegates to deal with the smaller matters. These delegates would range from responsibility for fifty people to thousands and ultimately the larger issues unable to be handled by the "regional" judges would be brought to Moses. Moses listens to the advice and implements the system which worked out very well. Jethro then leaves to go home.

There are three key principles we can glean from this story. The first is that success does not mean you cannot or should not improve. Moses and the nation of Israel had been through a series of victories through God's protection and deliverance. They were seeing miracles from the Red Sea crossing to water coming out of a rock to victory in war with the Amalekites. The judgment process that Moses had put together was working; however, it was not sustainable. It needed improvement. Sustainable success comes through continuous improvement. The second principle we can learn is that we must be open to learn from others (continuous learning). Jethro observed and pointed out the defects and came up with a viable solution. Moses listened to the advice because he had a willingness to learn. The third principle is there is power in effective delegation. Sometimes improving our processes, the way we work, etc. can be quickly done through the engagement of others such as delegating workload or responsibility. With further analysis, there are many other principles to glean from this story; however, we will leave that for your challenge to uncover.

Throughout the pages of Scripture, we can find examples of where people improved their ways of life, where God taught the value of learning (thereby by improving one's knowledge), and where God asks us to work hard *as unto Christ*. When we think of continuous improvement and the Bible, there are two critical truths we can apply to our own lives to help us in this area. The first truth has been spoken about in the earlier chapter on improving the customer experience. It was one of the CE action principles called the E910 principle. It is taken from the book of Ecclesiastes where King Solomon writes, "whatever your hand finds to do, do it with your might..."[155] A Scripture we reviewed earlier that builds upon this is found in Colossians where the apostle Paul writes, "whatever you do, work heartily, as for the Lord and not for men."[156] The truth is simply this: *God expects us to give our best in all things (including work) because we are serving Him in the process.* This means every report you develop, every meeting you run, every coffee drink you make, every customer you greet, every product you make, every service you provide, everything must be done to the best of your ability. The sooner we understand and apply this truth, the better our job performance will be. Be careful of the intentions behind giving your best. Theologian and Pastor A.W. Tozer writes, "Let every man abide in the calling wherein he is called and his work will be as sacred as the work of ministry. It is not what a man does that determines whether his work is sacred or secular, it is why he does it. The motive is everything. Let a man sanctify the Lord God in his heart and he can thereafter do no common act."[157]As stated in this biblical truth, our first and primary intention for excellence should be to serve Christ. Career growth, reward and recognition, and other results may come as a direct result of your high performance, but those should be secondary intentions. Giving our best means we need to continue to improve our knowledge and our skills which leads to the second critical truth.

Any brief study of the book of Proverbs will reveal God's passion and desire for us to learn and continue to grow in knowledge and wisdom. God gives us the foundation of knowledge when he states, "The fear of the Lord is the beginning of knowledge: but fools despise wisdom and instruction."[158] The fear of God is the foundation of knowledge because without God, we would not be created to begin with. Another verse states, "The fear of the Lord is the beginning of wisdom: and the knowledge of the Holy is understanding."[159] It all begins with God.

A.W. Tozer opens his wonderful book on the Knowledge of the Holy with, "what comes to our minds when we think about God is the most important thing about us."[160] This statement is profound. What comes to your mind when you think about God? The deeper we get in our relationship with him, the more the answer changes over time. If our answer is shallow, our relationship with God is most likely shallow. In fact, Tozer's book is a great place to start building your knowledge of the holy (of course the Bible is the primary source).

Realizing that God is the author and foundation for knowledge is key to our success in the workplace as Christians. Because this means all knowledge. God understands accounting procedures better than any accountant. He understands law better than any lawyer. God knows medicine better than any doctor. He knows education, public service, politics, military, finance, banking, construction, manufacturing, healthcare, and any other industry *better* than all human minds can fathom. If we start with growing in our knowledge of him, we will open ourselves to let God lead us in every area of life with trust and confidence. The second critical truth is this: *God desires us to continue in learning that we might continuously improve in all areas of life.* Throughout Proverbs we are exhorted to grow in knowledge and wisdom and are told where wisdom lengthens life, provides support, build confidence, and helps us avoid mistakes and sin. There are reasons for this. God longs for us to improve. First and foremost, he longs for our worship and love towards him. Our worship and love for him must grow to be fruitful. Secondly, we must grow in other areas of life including work. God tells us that in all labor there is profit.[161] The verse continues to say that the talk of the lips tends only to poverty. Growth requires action, improvement. When a crop is planted, a good farmer does everything he can to ensure a healthy, productive crop. He maintains the soil nutrients, knows when to plant and harvest, studies various tools, machinery and processes to improve his yield. All of this requires action through learning.

It is my hope that you begin to perform to the best of your ability in everything you do then position yourself to learn continuously. These two principles will be a sure foundation to establishing a continuous improvement mindset.

In Summary:

What is your experience with continuous improvement? Is it good or bad? Why?

_____

_____

_____

_____

_____

Name three business improvements that have impacted your life in the last five years. Do you wish to go back to the "good ole days"?

_____

_____

_____

_____

_____

What did you learn from the overview of 5S? How could you apply it to your workplace or job?

_____

_____

_____

_____

What did you learn from the overview of DMAIC? How could you apply it to your workplace or job?

_____

_____

_____

_____

What did you learn from the story of Moses and Jethro? What can you apply to your workplace or job?

_____

_____

_____

_____

_____

Several biblical principles and truths were discussed. Which one stood out to you? Why?

_____

_____

_____

_____

_____

Sample prayer for guidance on Continuous Improvement:

> *Lord Jesus, Thank you for knowledge. Thank you for the ability to learn and to improve. Grant me discipline, fortitude, strength and perseverance to grow in the knowledge of the Holy. Help me to grow in the workplace and to learn to work as unto you. Give me determination to work hard and give my best in all I do with the right intention of pleasing you. Open my mind and heart to learning opportunities that will enhance my performance and teach me continuous improvement daily.*
>
> *Amen.*

Chapter 8

God Invented Creativity, so what can we Learn from the Bible?

A recent *Newsweek* magazine article[162] on Creativity in America states, "a recent IBM poll of 1500 CEOs identified creativity as the number one 'leadership competency' of the future." The article also writes about the analysis of 300,000 Torrance scores (a measurement system for creativity in individuals used in all areas of the world) and how the findings show a decline in creativity in America, especially in younger children in elementary school. The importance of Creativity is becoming more and more apparent in all areas of life, especially in the workplace. As the IBM study indicates, it will be the number one competency in the future. How do you build creative skills individually, organizationally? Recognizing its importance, how do we become more creative in life, including at work? We will briefly explore best practices from global companies and biblical truths we can apply to become more creative. After all, God invented creativity.

If you were asked when you think about creativity what company comes to mind, what would your response be? Depending on where you are located in the world, the answer may or may not be different. Companies known for creativity include Apple, Google, Starbucks, Microsoft, and many others. There are others globally as well. Take for instance these three companies: Nanoco Technologies, Nano Retina and Impire.

According to a recent *CNBC Magazine* article[163] on Europe's twenty-five most creative companies, these three companies came in ranked at first, eighth, and ninth respectively. The brief background on each given in the article is fascinating. In first place, was Nanoco Technologies. Located in the U.K., Nanoco Technologies uses quantum dots technology. The article states, "Most of us probably won't get as excited about quantum dots—the nanoparticles of a semiconductor material, about 80,000 times thinner than human hair—as Michael Edelman or Nigel Pickett, but we will all benefit from the work these two scientists have been doing in Manchester, England. Semiconductors are the cornerstone of modern electronics. Quantum dots' conducting characteristics are closely linked to the size and shape of the individual crystal; as they are so small they display unique optical and electrical properties. This means that backlit LCD displays in computer screens—go on, feel how hot your screen is now—television sets and phones can be far more efficient and save energy; in lighting, quantum dots allow the colour of the light from a source to be precisely controlled."

Last September, Nanoco signed a joint development deal with a major television manufacturer, and Edelman says the first enhanced models should enter production next year. With legislation to reduce power consumption stalking the globe, quantum dots could suddenly be very big indeed. In fact, in order to meet growing demand, Edelman says that around three tonnes of quantum dots will be needed each year by 2012. Having cracked mass production for these little beauties, Nanoco is sitting pretty. What's more, quantum dots have traditionally been made with metals such as cadmium, which is now banned in consumer products; Nanoco has devised ways to produce cadmium-free quantum dots. The potential uses for the technology are exploding too. Edelman says quantum dots can also be used in photovoltaic (PV) panels to make solar power more efficient: "It's all about costs. The energy produced now for solar costs 2.4 cents per watt compared to sixty cents from a wall socket." In June, Nanoco struck its first commercial solar deal, signing an agreement with Tokyo Electron to develop a solar PV nanomaterial film for solar cell manufacturing equipment. Quantum dots could also build quantum computers, which work in a fundamentally different way to traditional ones; while the potential in various fields of medicine is also massive, with quantum dots being used with fibre-optic probes to distinguish between good and bad tissues. In its last financial year, Nanoco received a $2m as part of a $10m agreement with a major Japanese manufacturer, which produces LEDs for the general lighting and LCD backlight market. Nanoco expects to get the remaining $8m by the end of 2010. "We're experts on materials, not devices, so we strike strategic partnerships. The business model is working closely with partners who pay towards development cost, then again at the license agreement stage and then a small royalty on products sold that contains our patented technology." Nanoco's broker, Zeus Capital, forecasts that for 2010 and 2011, the company will generate €6m and €12m of revenues before a dazzling leap to €95m in 2012. Creativity can lead to exponential results.

Next is the eighth place Israeli company, Nano Retina. The article states, "In the U.S. alone, an estimated 3.6 million sufferers of degeneration of the retina (the membrane that lines the inside of the eyeball and is connected to the brain by the optic nerve) are legally blind. There is no known cure for the loss of function of the retina's photoreceptors, which may be caused by ageing or diabetes, and it is the second largest cause of blindness after cataract. Nano Retina thinks it has an answer for them and millions of others. Based in Herzliya, north of Tel Aviv, the small Israeli firm is developing a bionic retina, which managing director Ra'anan Gefen says 'is designed to restore full sight, by replacing the damaged photoreceptors with artificial ones.' The device consists of a tiny imager, similar to that used a digital camera, and an electronic interface with the eye's neurons encapsulated in a 5mm implant that can be embedded in a thirty-minute operation. The only external part is a wireless power source, attached to a pair of eyeglasses. Development by the firm, owned by Israeli investment firm Rainbow Medical and nanotech specialist Zyvex Labs of Dallas, is in an early stage, but the goal—which Gefen says includes the ability to recognise faces and watch TV—may be in sight. The first human trial of an implant is expected within three years, with clinical trials and commercial availability a couple of years more distant. For millions, that's still an encouraging vision."

Regarding the ninth most creative company in Europe, the article goes on to state, "… Using Impire data of more than 100,000 fouls—including seven seasons of Germany's Bundesliga (85,262 fouls) and the Champions League (32,142), and three World Cups (6,440)— two scientists at Rotterdam School of Management have proved that tall players such as England forward Peter Crouch (2.01m) will more often get penalised in a 50-50 clash with smaller players such as German defender Philipp Lahm (1.70m). Impire captures statistical data on every aspect of a game and turns it into real-time services. Future applications include real-time 3D game simulations, which viewers can follow from any player's perspective. Add in player avatars and these could offer an enhanced viewing experience, since fans can put themselves in any position on the pitch, making sports truly interactive and immersive."

What criteria do these companies have in common? The article says it's the disruptive force of their ideas. If we dig deep into any of the companies considered most creative on any continent and in any region and you will find several reasons for their ability to be creative. Three critical factors companies use to be successful at being creative are fostering environments/ processes for creative input, building idea generation at all levels of the organization, and driving execution on ideas to deliver results. In the U.S., 3M is often used as an example for being a creative company. Much has been written about their approach to enabling creativity in their employees. The same can be said for Google who allows employees to allocate a portion of time for innovation and creative thinking. Innovation can be learned and developed into a systematic process. Peter Drucker states, "...Innovation isn't inspired by a bright idea, rather it 'is organized, systematic, rational work.' Innovation can be mastered and integrated into a company or non-profit organization."[164] In the research I have done, each of the companies mentioned above, both global and U.S. based, are successful at these three factors. Fostering input, building ideas consistently and driving results from those ideas enable companies to be at the creative forefront.

What does fostering an environment for creativity mean? This includes empowering employees to be creative at work including simple things such as workspace layout or design, or the allocation of time for innovation training and brainstorming activities. A side note regarding brainstorming. Sometimes this methodology is not always effective. Many ideas or creative thoughts come from individual contributions and not in a brainstorming session. For example, if you wanted more creativity in the customer experience for your company's products or services, one way to foster creativity is to assign an afternoon where employees can leave work and go to several companies in their communities where they believe the customer experience is high. An employee can visit several

Starbucks in the area and monitor the Barista's approach to each customer. Employees can schedule meetings with local hotel management (think Four Seasons, Ritz Carlton or J.W. Marriott) asking to benchmark their customer experience in exchange for a coffee or meal. The idea is to change the setting, renew the focus, force vision from another company's lens on the customer experience. The following morning, you can have each employee present their findings including strengths and weaknesses of their visits and how they may apply them to their current role. Another effective way for fostering creativity is to invest in your people to attend formal conferences on innovation from time to time. This will require time and financial resources but the ROI can be significant in higher employee morale, increased productivity, idea generation improvement and overall employee satisfaction.

Another idea that would achieve both fostering an environment and idea generation would be to develop cross-functional *CreativeThink*Teams. Establish cross-functional teams of six to eight employees from at least five different areas of the organization and have them generate ideas, concepts and potential solutions for future growth in any number of areas. Establish team governance and procedures and set a time table. Include milestone checkpoints and conclude with a presentation to an executive committee where the winning team receives recognition. You can establish career guidelines and goals for participation in *CreativeThink*Teams as an option. Be creative with this idea. An excellent example of something like this is found in Boise, Idaho. Boise State business professor and executive director for Boise State's Centre for Creativity and Innovation, Nancy Napier, brought together a group of leaders in the Boise area who meet bi-monthly and are known as "The Gang." This group of eight leaders meets regularly and consists of a college football head coach (Chris Petersen of Boise State), a ballet dancer, a sheriff, a software engineer as well as others. Coach Petersen states in a recent article, "I started realizing game-plan wise, there wasn't enough creativity. I started looking at things a different way. We need structure, we need order, we need schedules, and we need our systems taught a certain way. But within that there needs to be a creativity to keep growing, to keep the energy and the enthusiasm."[165] Through meeting with other creative leaders from all walks of life, Coach Petersen learned how to be more creative. Our departments, divisions, and organizations can achieve the same goal using the same type of approach. The human mind is a powerful tool and when combined together with other minds, teams can be unstoppable.

There are other ways to build ideas within an organization. Unfortunately, companies sometimes put out the token "suggestion box" and assume all will be well with idea generation. More often than not the suggestion box does not yield sustainable idea generation. There are better ways. For example, you could develop "idea days" where certain activities could be done to promote generation of ideas. Plan for a Wednesday to be an idea day and schedule several brainstorming sessions throughout the day along with competitive activities to generate interest. You could use learning tools and educate employees on idea generation. You could conduct team competitions such as building the best paper airplanes and the team with the airplane that flies the longest, straightest, etc. will be recognized. They can also identify what ideas they came up with and how. Again, be creative with idea generation.

The third factor driving success for creativity at companies is driving specific results from the generation of ideas. There must be a formal process developed to capture, prioritize, analyze and test ideas that could turn to potential solutions.

This is typically where the "suggestion box" breaks down. Who collects from each box? What do they do with the info? How do you know if the interpretation of the suggestion is correct? Were you able to collect first person feedback? In order to deliver results from idea generation consistently, this process must collect the ideas in a formal manner with specific data requirements. A prioritization tool needs to be developed to enable effective prioritization of ideas; the good, the bad and the ugly so to speak. Energy spent on bad ideas is wasted energy once pursued. The prioritization stands each idea up to several standards selectively chosen, such as is the idea in-line with the company vision and core values, does it meet profitability targets, is it simple to develop, is it revenue generating, and so on. Tools such as the Pugh Matrix and others can help put weightings and rankings to each idea.

Once prioritization is complete, developing the ideas through deeper analysis is critical. At this stage, you are vetting out the details of the proposed idea. What risks are there? Costs? How fast should we go to market? These and many other questions are answered during this stage. Piloting the idea is the next stage and is critical for success. Successful pilots reveal both strengths and weaknesses in the idea. Testing through piloting allows for the idea to fail in a controlled environment. It also builds confidence back in the idea generation phase as employees will not feel as anxious with risking action from an idea. Once the pilot is successful and all learning is done, the idea, now a solution, can move forward into mainstream production.

We have learned what other companies and organizations have done to successfully drive creativity. Fostering an environment where creativity can flourish is key. Building ideas consistently over time is also key to success. However, it does not stop with these two factors. Focusing on delivering real solutions from ideas also fosters an environment of creativity therefore driving more idea generation. It is cyclical when done properly.

What does the Bible say about creativity? The Bible has plenty to say about creativity because God developed creativity and is the master innovator. There are several principles we can glean from the Word of God that will enable us to be more creative in our lives while also encouraging others to do so.

The first principle we can learn is that God built us with a sense of wonder. Unfortunately, over the span of human history, humanity is losing its sense of wonder, but is this biblical? Why is it important to have a sense of wonder? These questions and their answers will frame up our first principle: Renew a sense of wonder, starting with Christ. Plato once stated that all philosophy begins with wonder. I would expand that to say all of human life begins with wonder. Think back to your childhood. There were times in your life that were filled with wonder, a sense of awe that could not be explained. Christmas mornings when waiting to open gifts, starry skies filled with lights and darkness, animals we never saw before right before us in the zoo, and as a boy, I was filled with wonder pretending to be a top motocross rider riding around a make believe track. After reflecting on your life, have you lost a bit of wonder? Francis Bacon stated that wonder dies with knowledge. There is much truth to this statement except in one thing: our wonder of God. Why? Because we will never know everything (or even close to everything) about God until we are with him in heaven. So that leaves room for wonder.

We are to reflect on Christ and God our heavenly father with awesome respect and wonder. King David wrote, "…when I consider thy heavens, the work of thy fingers, the moon and the stars, which thou hast ordained; what is man, that thou art mindful of him? And the son of man, that thou visitest him?... O Lord our Lord, how excellent is thy name in all the earth."[166] David understood this sense of wonder. Matthew Henry, Theologian in the eighteenth century, writes on this passage, "when we consider how the glory of God shines in the upper world we may well wonder that he should take cognizance of such a mean creature as man, that he who resides in that bright and blessed part of the creation, and governs it, should humble himself to behold the things done upon this earth."[167] There are many other examples where David had this sense of wonder about God. The book of Psalms is filled with the thoughts of David towards his awesome God. David was not perfect by any means; however, the Bible says he was a man after God's own heart. David led a very successful life and God blessed him in many ways. I believe part of the reason David was so successful was that he never lost his sense of wonder (sometimes fearful wonder) towards God. David even recognized God's sovereignty in his being stating that he was fearfully and wonderfully made.[168] When was the last time you truly had a sense of awe about Christ? Have you truly thought about how God created the heavens and the earth, then mankind, then womankind, and when all seemed lost through rebellious sin, God provided the ultimate wonder found in his son, Jesus Christ? This is truly wonderful.

The more we grow in our relationship with Christ, the more our wonder grows of him. And when this happens, we are more open to his creative purposes for our lives. Ravi Zacharias writes, "God is like light. Wonder is like the shadow. If you chase the shadow you will never catch up to it. It might even disappear. If you walk toward the light, the shadow will always pursue you. That is when the heart sings with gladness."[169] Renewing a sense of wonder will open your mind for greater things. Nature has a way of giving us a sense of wonder as well, (funny how God's creation gives us wonder) so spending time in nature will also open your mind to creative opportunities. Have you ever stood on the edge of the Grand Canyon? Have you ever witnessed the power of the ocean during storms? Have you truly understood the great migrations of animals that take place every year all over the planet? Millions of creatures, from bats to birds to wildebeests, migrate hundreds and thousands of miles every year. All of these things and many more should create a sense of wonder. Elizabeth Barrett Browning writes a few lines that sum up a key message around this:

> Earth's crammed with heaven,
> and every common bush afire with God
> But only he who sees, takes off his shoes
> The rest sit around it and pluck blackberries.[170]

After spending time renewing your sense of wonder, the next biblical principle is the practice of the disciplines of worship and prayer. Through our authentic worship, we become submissive to God's will for our lives. We also become open to direction. Ravi Zacharias goes on to write, "when we have learned what worship is, we have experienced what wonder is."[171] Worship is a disciplined act. We must first discipline ourselves to worship before it becomes a way of life for us. Our sinful nature does not want to worship the King of Kings. This takes practice and not just on Sundays or whatever your day of worship and gathering is. Thomas Carlyle wrote, "Worship is transcendent wonder."[172] How deeply do you worship in your everyday life? Do you feel its transcendent? This is the purpose of man in simple form. We are saved through Christ so that we can worship Christ, voluntarily and willingly. A.W. Tozer writes, "When a man falls on his knees and stretches his hands heavenward, he is doing the most natural thing in the world. Something deep within compels him to seek someone or something outside of himself to worship and adore. In his unredeemed condition, man has lost the way and cannot clearly define the object of his wistful adoration, and so his search takes him far from God. When he does not find God, man will fill the void in his heart with anything he can find. That which is not God can never satiate the heart exclusively created for God's presence."[173] If you practice the discipline of authentic worship, you will find yourself being more creative in life as God fills you with his purpose.

Earlier in this book, we discussed the spiritual disciplines and the importance of prayer. Specific prayers for improved creativity such as "Lord Jesus, we need a fresh set of ideas for our department. I am open to your wisdom and knowledge. Teach me to be alert, aware and open to ideas throughout each coming day" can go a long way in helping us to become more creative. Too often, Christians are afraid to pray for these types of things or perhaps they simply don't know how. Prayer is a conversation with our heavenly father who wants to give us the desires of our heart (motive is key here). Praying for improved creative minds should not be abnormal but a norm for Christians. James tells us in his book that the fervent prayer of a righteous man accomplishes much.[174] This includes every area of our lives where we want to see God glorified. We should pray that God is glorified through our hard work and continuous learning. Prayer accomplishes much!

In review, creativity sets man apart from other creatures. God instilled innovation in us. Through specific actions such as fostering environments of creativity, generating ideas consistently and delivering results from those ideas, we can become better at what we do thereby giving us a platform to do more good in the name of Christ.

In Summary:

What is the most creative thing you have ever seen to date (could be any area of life)? Why?

_____

_____

_____

_____

_____

Why is creativity (or being creative) so hard sometimes?

_____

_____

_____

_____

_____

What can you do to foster an environment of creativity?

_____

_____

_____

_____

_____

Do you feel you have a strong sense of wonder, especially for God? If so, why? If not, why not?

_____

_____

_____

_____

If worship is our purpose, do you feel you are achieving the purpose in your personal life?

_____

_____

_____

_____

_____

Write down three areas in your life you feel you need to be more creative in (one must be work related). Now pray for these three areas every day for thirty days. Journal your progress.

_____

_____

_____

_____

_____

Sample prayer for guidance on Creativity:

> *Lord, I praise you for who you are. I thank you for being a creative God. Renew a sense of wonder for your love in my life. Help me to focus on your word and speak to me through it. As I focus more on you, teach me to be more creative in my life. Give me learning opportunities and open my mind to new ideas and fresh thoughts. Help me to apply and deliver results. In all of this, may your glory be revealed.*
>
> *Amen.*

Chapter 9

Sustainability: Caretaking God's Creation

A simple definition for sustainability is a measure of the balance between environmental resource consumption and the impact of man-made products and how sustainable both are for future generations. As the world's needs continue to expand, the impact on our resources continues to accelerate. A few facts on the wages of success.[175]

- Industrial Waste—The U.S. economy consumes over one hundred billion tons of raw materials per year; more than 90 percent of this ends up as waste which equals one ton of waste per person per day.

- In the U.S., 93 percent of plastics end up in landfills

- Regenerative (Renewable) Resources:

    o One-fifth of the world's people do not have reliable access to clean drinking water

    o Overproduction of topsoil has caused severe or extreme soil degradation of over two and a half billion acres (more than the size of China and India combined)

    o Over 70 percent of the world's fisheries are chronically overfished

    o More than a third of the world's forests have disappeared in the last fifty years

Real sustainable workplace performance requires obtaining knowledge about the future of your industry/business, your customers, your suppliers and your fellow employees. All are affected by the above statistics. Christians are not exempt. As we'll explore, we are to care for the Earth as God's creation and the more we can all improve in this area, the better of our world will be and our workplaces as well. However, as with many things, there must be a balance. We are not to worship the Earth or the things within it. Only human beings are made in the image of God;[176] not trees, not animals, not anything else. This is a fundamental difference between secular (including evolution, naturalism, etc.) and creationist theories of how all of creation was formed. The Bible states that God created the Earth and Heavens and that he also created mankind. With this belief, a person should not be careless in managing God's resources if they truly believe everything was created by Him.

Just because humanity is made in the image of God however, does not give mankind the right to abuse the resources of the Earth. More important, we should take care of the resources so they can be used for future generations. President Theodore Roosevelt once quipped the nation behaves well if it treats the natural resources as assets which it must turn over to the next generation increased, and not impaired in value. President Roosevelt had it right. From generation to generation, we should be improving the sustainable use of natural resources.

So what does the Bible say about God and the Earth? In one of the oldest books of the Bible, the book of Job, the author tells us that during his last response to Job God stated that whatsoever is under the whole heaven is mine.[177] God claims sole ownership of everything, all of space, all universes, time and everything related to it. God owns it all. King David writes in one of his Psalms that the earth is the Lord's, and the fullness thereof;

the world, and they that dwell therein.[178] David recognizes the ownership of the Earth belongs to God including those that inhabit the planet. Some 400-500 years earlier, Moses writes that the heavens and the heaven of heavens including the Earth also belong to God.[179]

It's not just the older books or the Old Testament that claims God owns everything including the Earth. The New Testament also claims this as well. Paul repeats King David's statement in his first letter to the church at Corinth stating the Earth is the Lord's, and the fullness thereof.[180] In doing so, the apostle Paul validates what David wrote. The apostle Paul also writes of how Christ created all things. In his letter to the Colossians, Paul writes, "For by him (Christ) all things were created, in heaven and on earth, visible and invisible, whether thrones or dominions or rulers or authorities—all things were created through him and for him. And he is before all things, and in him all things hold together."[181] We have established the fact of God's ownership of the Heavens and Earth through the validation of the Word of God. It does not stop here. God also shares that he cares for the Earth and commands us to do just that as well. In speaking of the Promised Land, Moses tells us that God cared for the land.[182] The tax collector and Apostle, Matthew, documented Christ's Sermon on the Mount. In this powerful sermon (some consider the most powerful given), Jesus Christ gives us a picture of the caretaking of God for the Earth. While speaking about anxiety and worry, Christ tells us not worry about what we will eat or drink or how we will be clothed. He tells us that the birds of the air don't sow and reap yet they are fed by God himself. Christ also tells us to consider the lilies of the field. These lilies do not work or sow yet they are clothed in splendor. If God cares for the birds and for flowers, how much more will he care for us? This was the context Christ was speaking in.[183] Let's not miss this. Jesus tells us himself that God feeds the birds and that he has "clothed" the fields. God is the ultimate caretaker of his glorious garden, the Earth.

His expectation of us is no less. He commanded Adam and Eve to be fruitful, multiply and replenish the Earth.[184] Adam and Eve were to make use of the Earth's resources; however, because they are made in the image of God (as stated one verse earlier) it is implied they would do so responsibly as God himself cares for his creation. This commandment did not give Adam and Eve the right to exploit the Earth and its resources for greedy gains. As one commentator writes, "Man would fill the earth and oversee its operation. Subdue does not suggest a wild and unruly condition for the creation because God himself pronounced it good."[185]

Now that we have validated God's ownership of everything including the earth and our responsibility to care for all of creation, there are several principles we can glean from the Bible. The first principle is in the form of a question. If God created the Earth and it was good, then do we believe that it is good (to be taken care of)? God clearly stated his creation of mankind, creation and the Earth was good. If we really believed God felt his work was "good" shouldn't we? This simple concept of believing that creation is good builds a foundation for us to grow on. The goodness of God shows in his creation. I believe the goodness of God resides in nature, but let's be careful here. Nature should never be worshipped as we stated before. We should worship the Creator and not the creation. In doing so, God will give us new appreciation for his creation. The second principle is because the earth is the Lord's, we should *want* to take care of it. Once we believe that God did create a *good* earth, this should lead us to want to take care of his creation.

Again, careful balance must be given here. The earth was given to humanity by God and he commanded us to be fruitful and multiply and replenish the earth. This gave us permission to use the earth's resources for the good of mankind. Many in society today believe we should not be using trees, oil, minerals, and other natural resources due to the "damage" we create. This is not the intention of God. God's intention was for us to use resources in a responsible, sustainable way. The third principle is since God cares for creation, then we should follow his example. Our paradigms need to change. Extremists on both sides of the use of natural resources have it wrong. If we changed our paradigm to caring like God cares, the earth and everything in it would be a much better place. Could you imagine God ripping up trees irresponsibly? Can you imagine God filling the skies with carbon emissions without an alternative sustainable approach? Would God place natural resources above humanity? Does He think a beetle's life is worth as much as a human life? Of course not. God cares for His creation as should we, but He also places special care and love on the only creature made in His image, human beings. Through really caring as the God of the universe does, we understand we have a responsibility to take care of the earth and to pass along to future generations better renewable resource management.

What can we do? Start out by taking small steps. Several examples include turning off the water while brushing your teeth. Use a container with a filter to refill water instead of purchasing water bottles, recycle-recycle-recycle, use less electricity (use natural light, monitor air conditioning/heating usage, etc.), and the best step is to pray (pray for others less fortunate without natural resources). Be specific in your prayers, focusing on sustainability from time to time.

By now you may be asking what does this have to do with my job? Good question. It is important to set a foundation and establish the principles before discussing what we can do on the job. Why? Because if we truly believe in and adhere to the principles explained earlier, then our actions at work will be all the more open to sustainable approaches and processes. As leaders and believers in the workplace, we need to set the example. Simple actions that could be taken at work include engaging your team members and/or employees in sustainability activities (external to office if possible). Perhaps you and others can help clear hiking paths, clean up some parks/beaches, work with local environmental groups on education, etc. You could even approach sustainability within the office. Does your company have a recycling process? If not, establish one. Does your company educate its employees on sustainable processes? If not, establish a training program. Perhaps you can start a lunch time book club where once a week or month (timeframe is up to you) a group can read through a book on sustainability and discuss their opinions about the messages, facts and data from the book. No matter what you choose to do, the idea is not to take away from productivity but through these events and actions productivity may be improved as everyone focuses on a common purpose. If you are really serious, you could implement the Joint Sustainability Model. This model is a simple way to engage many different resources following a simple five step process. Step one is to conduct industry research, step two is to create a focus group, three is to develop employees, step four is to develop a Joint Sustainability Team (JST), and step five is to measure for results. As we briefly review what each step means and what actions are needed, begin to think about the application of this model in your workplace.

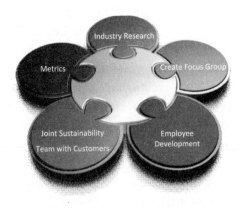

Step one of the Joint Sustainability Model is to conduct industry research. What is happening with sustainability in your industry? In your community? In other industries? These questions and more should be answered during this step. Many industries already have sustainable practices in them. Through understanding these practices, you begin to establish a baseline from which to launch your sustainable activities. For example, in the technology industry, specifically the printer sector, HP, Dell, Xerox and Lexmark, all have sustainable practices in place. Xerox is a strong leader in this space and its emphasis on sustainable improvement during research and development is world class. Peter Senge recognizes Xerox's leadership in his recent excellent book on sustainability titled *The Necessary Revolution.*[186] Xerox focuses on continuous improvement of solid waste reduction from its toners and inks, printer components, etc. Carbon emissions and energy utilization reduction is also measured and targeted for continuous improvement. In one customer recently, we saw more than a 20 percent reduction in energy and solid waste as we implemented a services-based solution. Through understanding the practices in your respective industries, you can learn to leverage or benchmark what others are doing as well as understand how the market is measuring for success in this area. During this step you are also gathering facts and data to be used in developing an educational/training program if not already developed. An excellent source is through LEED or the Leadership of Energy and Environmental Design certification process developed by the U.S. Green Building Council. According to Wiki.Org sources, LEED is an internationally recognized green building certification system, providing third-party verification that a building or community was designed and built using strategies intended to improve performance in metrics such as energy savings, water efficiency, CO_2 emissions reduction, improved indoor environmental quality, and stewardship of resources and sensitivity to their impacts.[187]

Step two is to create a focus group. The purpose of the focus group is to organize data collection, awareness training, activities, reporting, etc. This does not have to be a formal team. You could start out with just your fellow co-workers. Groups of people can provide great motivation for learning and getting results. To make it more effective, invite employees from different functions to serve on a sustainability focus group. There is power in cross functional teams. Some companies have departments dedicated to this area, like Xerox. Others may not. The key here is to engage in a team environment. This will help facilitate quality change if done correctly. The focus group could be rotational in participation allowing for everyone to get involved at some point without on-going time commitments. Regular meeting cadence is a must and meeting management skills must be used (time management, strong agendas, action tracking, etc.) in order for the team to be fruitful. Top down support is crucial to formal approaches but not necessarily needed in informal use of the model.

Step three is to develop employees. One of the objectives of the focus group could be to develop an awareness and/or training program for fellow employees in the company. The program could be as informal as educating employees on sustainable actions for the home and office or be as formal as creating certification levels for certain activities being completed including community service, office, home and other activities. Knowledge is power as the old saying goes. Educating employees and others around you can create exponential power for sustainable improvement.

Step four is to develop a JST (Joint Sustainability Team) with key partners, suppliers, competitors and/or customers. This is a very formal step that can yield great results and show real value to all involved. Many companies are already doing this in some form or fashion. In the age of outsourcing, most large corporations have many companies represented on-site throughout their enterprise. This is true globally. Many of these same companies have activities they promote throughout the year for sustainability. Employees from all parties are invited to participate many times. For example, in Seattle, a large asset management firm regularly schedules environmental improvement projects including clearing hiking trails and cleaning up parks. On several occasions, Xerox personnel have been invited and participated in these activities. Both companies benefited as did the projects they jointly worked together on. Step four is about formalizing this process. This five step model we are currently working through can be the same model this team can use.

Step five is to measure for success. If you are not measuring for progress and results, you do not have an effective process in anything. This is a simple fact. Company objectives and targets are only as good as the metrics tracking them. If there is very little measurement, most goals and targets are never achieved or can never be proven. It's the same for this model. The effectiveness of this model is only as good as the metrics teams will develop to track their performance. These metrics will vary by industry, by company, and perhaps by individual (if done individually). The key is to choose the right measurement system and measure consistently. This does not mean analysis paralysis or death by data approaches. All too often, companies spend too much time on data mining and analysis when they don't need to.

There you have it. You may not choose to use the model. That's OK. However, choose to do something about sustainability and the use of our natural resources. When in doubt, pray. God will provide direction and wisdom no matter what you are struggling with regarding balancing a passion for His creation, the Earth. He has given us a magnificent planet to sustain human life. It is His gift to us. Let's pass the gift to future generations. The retired country music group, Alabama, sings a great song regarding this, titled "Pass It On Down." The lyrics are as follows: *We live in the land of plenty, but many things aren't plenty anymore, like the water from our sink they say it's not safe to drink, you gotta go and buy it at the store, now we're told there's a hole in the ozone, look what's washing on the beach, and Lord, I believe from the heavens to the seas, we're bringing mother nature to her knees, (chorus) so let's leave some blue up above us, let's leave some green on the ground, it's only ours to borrow let's save some for tomorrow, leave it and pass it on down. Well there's a change taking place way on the mountains, acid rain is falling on the leaves, and down in Brazil the fires are burning still, how we gonna breathe without them trees?, there's a place where I live called the Canyon, where daddy taught me to swim, and that water it's so pure and I'm gonna make sure, daddy's grandkids can swim there like him, now we all oughta feel just a little bit guilty, when we look into the eyes of our kids, 'cause brothers it's a fact, if we take and don't put back, they'll have to pay for all we did, so let's leave some blue up above us, let's leave some green on the ground, it's only ours to borrow let's save some for tomorrow, leave it and pass it on down.*[188]

In Summary:

What have you done in the last month to positively impact the environment around you?

_____

_____

_____

_____

_____

Have you prayed for others who are less fortunate with natural resources (clean water, etc)?

_____

_____

_____

_____

Do your peers and/or employees know that sustainability is important? If not, why?

_____

_____

_____

_____

_____

Have you studied what the Bible says about the Earth and its resources?

_____

_____

_____

_____

_____

We need to balance our love of nature and the importance of human life, both of which are created by God. Why are humans more important in God's overall creation?

_____

_____

_____

_____

_____

What three actions can you immediately take to support Sustainability?

_____

_____

_____

_____

_____

Sample prayer for guidance on Sustainability:

Lord, thank you for your creation. Thank you for the blessings you have given me as I enjoy the resources of your Earth. Please give me the ability to learn and the willingness to take action regarding taking care of your earth.

I pray for balance in my leadership, my company and my life. Help me to stay focused on you and allow you to use me however you will. Please intervene in the lives of those who are suffering due to a lack of natural resources. Help me to remember them in my daily prayer life. In your name,

Amen.

Chapter 10

In Conclusion: Keeping it Real

Though this is a book about job performance and workplace improvement using biblical principles, we need to be very careful that our work and all facets of it does not become the god of our lives. As we have discussed, the gift of work was given by God for purpose, fulfillment and the ability to be self-reliant. Work was created by God; however, work should not replace God. We need to keep it real and our lives balanced. This is why the spiritual disciplines are so important in our lives. Through these disciplines, we grow in our faith, our strength, and our relationship with Christ thereby directly impacting all areas of life as we allow God deeper access and control. We should pray as the Psalmist prayed, "Let the words of my mouth and the meditation of my heart be acceptable in thy sight O Lord my strength and my redeemer."[189] Our lives should be pleasing to God, keeping Him always first in our lives.

Christians tend to polarize themselves when it comes to work. On one end, you have those who have made work their daily god, some without even realizing it. These are the people who consistently work long hours (justifying it with reasons like career growth, etc.), who live for their careers, who work at home even after they come home from the office, who do not participate in community activities such as church because they are too busy. While at times, these activities are required, they should not be a long-term activity or approach. On the other end are those Christians who view work as just a source of income, a daily grind without real value. These are the people who justify mediocre work performance or giving "just enough" to get by because "after all, this is our temporary home."

God is the God of balance. He understands we need to balance our lives in Him and in all areas. He commanded us to be still and know that he is God.[190] He told us to trust in him and acknowledge him and he will direct our paths.[191] Only with his guidance, can we truly balance our lives in accordance with his will and purpose. In life, including our work, we are to be balanced so that we may be more effective. Our effectiveness can be impacted by out-of-balance factors influencing work and life. We will explore two of these factors and how to mitigate for them in our lives and specifically our jobs. The two factors (with potential actions to mitigate in parenthesis) are busyness or being controlled by time (manage and simplify) and complacency (getting results). I have specifically listed these in this order as throughout my career and experiences, I have seen these issues impact myself and others with greater proportion in this order. These factors impact all ages, all cultures, and span the globe. I have seen them firsthand in India, China, Korea, Japan, England, Ireland, France, Brazil, Switzerland, Israel, Canada, Mexico and in thirty-three plus states in the U.S.[192]

Busyness is a plague that has penetrated humanity and is growing exponentially year after year. While technology has certainly improved quality of life and overall productivity, it comes at a price. Sometimes, it comes at a very heavy price. Busyness is also the enemy of workplace performance. There is too much noise in the workplace today. People must process thousands of bits of data and information every day. It is quite common around the globe to have employees participating in virtual team meetings via conference call and at the same time, managing e-mails, and communicating through instant messaging resources, or answering other phone calls—we have phrased it "multi-tasking." While the ability to multi-task is a valuable skill, this variation of it can decrease productivity and overall efficiency. Studies have been done to prove so.[193]

The two greatest tools to combat busyness are time management and simplification. The Bible has plenty to say about both. We'll explore time management first. We are to be good managers of our time according to the Word of God.[194] King Solomon wrote there is a time and purpose for everything and then proceeds to give examples including times regarding laughter, crying, birth, death, war, peace, etc.[195] The key message in this portion of Scripture is that at certain points in life, we all deal with things that take time and are an integral part of our daily lives and we cannot change that. Commentator Matthew Henry writes of this portion of Scripture, "The scope of these verses is to show that every change concerning us, with time and season of it, is unalterably fixed and determined by a supreme power; and we must take things as they come, for it is not in our power to change what is appointed to us."[196] Recognizing that we have appointed changes during our life, we should be all the more ready to manage our time wisely. The ability to manage time can and should be learned. Time is the one thing humans cannot stop. Every second turns to a minute which turns to hours which then leads to days, weeks, months, years, decades, centuries, etc. God created time for a purpose and it is important that we manage our time according to his purposes and will.

There are many great resources on time management so the intent of this section is not to come up with new models or tools to use. The intent is to awaken a desire within the reader to want to manage their time better. There are 168 hours in a week and the question is how do we spend those hours? Are they productive? Do they serve the purpose of our lives? Do they add value to different areas of life (family, work, community, etc.)? These and other questions must be looked at when we analyze our time management. A great book on this topic is *168 Hours: You have more time than you think* published by Penguin Group.[197] In this book, the author, Laura Vanderkam, does a great job of showing the reader how effective one can be through the analysis and management of their 168 hours. Vanderkam shakes the paradigm of "not having enough time" through statistical analysis and time studies. Simple tools and processes are given to encourage the reader to conduct their own analysis and change their approach to managing their weeks. Time management is about prioritization. Stephen Covey used to demonstrate the importance of prioritization through the rocks, pebbles, sand and water story and later through demonstrations he gave in seminars.[198] He would take an empty glass jar and have a bunch of rocks (representing important things in our lives such as family, religion, etc.) to the side. He would then place the rocks in the jar, followed by pebbles (smaller priorities), then sand (little unimportant tasks, activities, interruptions), and finally he would add the water (pure time wasters). It all would fit into the jar. He would go on to say that many things fill our lives but if we let the smaller things fill our lives and time first, we would never get to the "rocks" or important things or have very little room for them.

In the earlier chapter on spiritual disciplines, the discipline of simplicity was discussed. As stated in that chapter, the essence of simplicity is found in the Scripture where Paul states that in whatever state I am in, I am content.[199] He can boldly make this statement because his real value and purpose is found in his relationship with Jesus Christ. Paul was content in his life and did not seek to add unnecessary noise including stress, fear, envy, etc. that may come with unnecessary activities in his life. If you truly live fully contented in life, a natural by-product is simplification. Why? Because a person truly contented with life in Christ does not look to fill the voids with meaningless noise. Instead, they look to fill the voids with service to God. In return, God keeps them in security and peace no matter what trials, struggles, and other things they may be facing. Simplicity breeds contentment and is most effective when done through Christ's commands. Of course this does not mean we don't slip into busyness from time to time or have made decisions that have added unnecessary complexity to our lives. Even sincere followers of Christ have issues at time with allowing or enabling too much complexity (or noise) in life. At times in my life, I have been involved with several organizations, played worship as a drummer, taught Bible studies among other activities at the same time all while trying to pursue career advancement, stay engaged with family and loving my wife and kids. While many of these activities were productive in and of themselves, I certainly was spread way too thin and due to my inability and/or unwillingness to simplify, I as well as my family paid the costs including lost time (never to be made up again). It is a regret I will go to the grave with.

Simplification in life takes discipline and three things have worked for me as I have learned to simplify over the years. The first thing is prioritizing my relationship with Christ above everything else. In making sure I spend time in his word daily, in daily prayer, and in fellowship with other followers, God has kept me balanced and content in my life even though I may be facing crisis at work or in my personal life. The second thing is to learn to say no. Many things in life will fill up your time. PTA participation, church activities, non-profit boards, sports, hobbies, entertainment, technology (TV, gaming, social media and internet as examples), sleep, health, food, work, family and friends all take up portions of our time (not an inclusive list). Our ability to say no to some of these activities even for short periods of time goes a long way to simplifying our lives. I have heard of many people taking media fasts where they eliminate the use of media for entertainment for a certain period of time and replace the activity with other activities such as solitude, or exercise, or face to face conversations with family and friends. I have done this many times myself. The average person, according to Nielsen, in America spends thirty hours per week watching television. Laura Vanderkam's studies show an average of eighteen to twenty-three hours per week per person.[200] Either way, that's a lot of time in front of a box. While I have never achieved these averages in my own life, I have eliminated television at times in my life for short periods of time (sometimes for a day or two and other times for a week or two). This practice alone opened my eyes to time I could be using more effectively. By simplifying my habits, I was able to read more—a passion of mine. Reflect on your time management for a moment. Think about how often you watch television in a week. Imagine if you took those hours and did not watch television. What other things would you do? Saying no to even the smallest activities or noise like this can simplify your life which could also positively impact your work life.

The second factor that can influence our life and create an out of balance culture is complacency. All too often, I have spoken with and witnessed people who are complacent in their jobs and many in almost every area of their lives. While there are many reasons that can enable complacent behaviors, there is no room for complacency in our lives. I have heard all of the excuses. "I am just not understood," "I have been too busy," "I don't get paid enough," "that's not my job," "I don't know how to do it," "I am not being treated fairly by management," and "we need more information" are all classic excuses that feed complacent behavior. Complacency breeds poor results. You must work to eliminate complacent behaviors in your life. One of the simple ways to do this is to achieve all of the goals in your life and at work. Think about this for a minute. Most of us have performance targets at work. Metrics like attendance, product completion, deadlines, sales targets, productivity, etc. Do you strive to achieve all of your goals at work? If not, reflect on why. Thinking more broadly, do you set goals in other areas of your life? Spiritual, educational, financial, personal (fitness), family and hobby goals are just several areas in which we should have goals. Complacent behaviors don't like goals. Instead they make excuses why goals cannot be achieved. You want to stop complacency in your life? Get results. Focus on goal achievement and you will not be complacent. Be cross functional in your goal setting. For example, I have set many goals throughout the years in my life. Some are longer term, some annual, some short-term goals. There have been years where I have set a goal to read the entire Bible in a year. This is not as easy as it may sound. At the same time, I have had goals to fish at least four to six times a year, speak at ministry opportunities, overachieve my performance targets at work, spend date nights with my wife, read at least four non-fiction books per year, and the list goes on. While I may not have achieved all of these goals at different times in my life, you can be certain I strived for it. And when you strive for goals, complacency cannot come in and take ownership. It's hard to be complacent as you are achieving goals in life.

Get results in the workplace. The E9:10 principle that we covered earlier in this book applies here as well. Whatever is in your hand, do with all your might.[201] Remember Schaeffer's quote, "If you do your work well, you will have a chance to speak." Besides working as unto Christ as we are commanded and giving our all as King Solomon writes in Ecclesiastes, this quote by Schaeffer should be the secondary reason why we should be getting results in the workplace. Your fellow team members, your partners, your customers, and your management should all hold the same opinion of you. They should all be saying he or she is hard working and fun, delivers results, walks in integrity and treats everyone with dignity and respect. At minimum. Strive to achieve this and watch complacency disappear. Do not be spiritually ignorant to the importance of finishing your work and ultimately your life well and strong. Lt. General Hal Moore writes, "We all should work, at any age, in any condition, if at all possible, to avoid floating about in spiritually devastating ignorance. We must have the heart to finish well, to finish strong."[202] He should know. Lt. General Moore led many soldiers into battle during the Vietnam War and was immensely respected and liked by his men. His leadership finished well and finished strong.

In Summary

In the classic devotional, *Evening by Evening*, Charles H. Spurgeon wrote the following. *Some people have the foolish notion that the only way in which they can live for God is by becoming pastors, missionaries, or Bible teachers. How many would be excluded from any opportunity of spiritual usefulness if this were the case. Beloved, it is not office—it is sincerity; it is not position—it is grace that will enable us to serve and glorify God. God is definitely glorified at the workbench, where the godly worker fulfills his task singing of the Savior's love. In this humble setting God is glorified far more than many a lofty pulpit where official religion performs its scanty duties. The name of Jesus is glorified by the taxicab driver as he blesses God and speaks to his passengers of the living hope. He will be more useful than the popular preacher who goes about peddling the Gospel for profit. God is glorified when we serve*

Him in our proper vocations. Take care, dear reader, that you do not neglect the path of duty by leaving your occupation, and take care you do not dishonor your profession while in it. Every lawful trade may be sanctified by the Gospel to noblest ends. Turn to the Bible and you will find the most menial forms of labor connected either with the most daring deeds of faith or with persons whose lives have been illustrations of holiness. Therefore do not be discontented with your calling. Whatever God has made your position at work, remain in that, unless you are quite sure that He calls you to something else. Let your first concern be to glorify God to the best of your ability where you are. Fill your present sphere to His praise, and if He needs you in another, He will show it to you[203]...

Spurgeon is absolutely correct. Our jobs, our workplaces, and our careers are ministries God has placed us in. Once we understand the value of work and how God views it, we can gain a whole new perspective and in turn live a deeper life of purpose. The practice of spiritual disciplines in our lives enables us to grow and deepen the biblical worldview internally. These disciplines open our hearts to the Creator of the universe and to the Savior of our souls. In return, His Word penetrates our hearts, minds and souls[204] and we become true followers of Christ. Unfortunately, we live in a world today that is losing its knowledge of biblical doctrine and Christian facts and therefore do not understand the importance of disciplines and having a close relationship with Christ including in-depth knowledge of His Word. In a recent U.S. based survey conducted by the Pew Forum on Religion and Public life[205] revealed startling results. Seventy-one percent polled correctly stated Jesus was born in Bethlehem. That means 29 percent of Americans did not know Jesus was born in Bethlehem. Another statistic shows 63 percent correctly named Genesis as the first book in the Bible. Again, this means 37 percent of Americans did not know Genesis was the first book in the Bible. The survey also found that only 37 percent of Americans say they read the Bible at least *once a week*. This is a really sad statistic. While most Americans claim to be Christians, only 37 percent read the Word of God. We wonder why we have seen a growing lack of understanding of our faith? Is it really any wonder that people have a hard time grasping how to integrate their faith at work when many don't understand the Bible (and its central faith building tenets and doctrines)? It is time to grow in our relationship with Christ. It is time to put Him first.[206] It is time to be disciplined and commit to reading and hearing from God's Word. In doing so, we will reap exponential benefits and rewards in this life and in eternal life.

Once we have come to terms with the need to be growing as a Christian, we can then ask God to help us grow in our workplaces and careers. Your job should not be a place of stagnant growth. Growth comes through performance. Being a Christian is no excuse for average or poor workplace performance. God expects more. He expects us to perform to the best of our ability as unto Him and Him alone. If for no other reason, this should cause us to be high performers in the workplace. We should pray as the Psalmist prayed, "Let the words of my mouth and the meditations of my heart be acceptable." The Bible is relevant to the workplace. We can learn principles, concepts, examples and commands that we can and should use in daily work that will improve our job performance and in time the performance of our companies and businesses. Are you allowing the Bible to be relevant in every area of your life? What if someone were to interview your customers, peers, suppliers and/or your management? Would they say you lived out the biblical view of work? The proof is in your job performance.

Endnotes

1   Patrick Morley, *A Man's Guide to Work* (Chicago: Moody Publishers, 2010), 83.

2   Faith, for the purposes of this writing, refers to Christianity unless otherwise noted.

3   David W. Miller, *God at Work; the History and Promise of the Faith at Work Movement* (New York: Oxford University Press, 2007).

4   Max Weber, *The Protestant Ethic and the Spirit of Capitalism* 1930 English translation.

5   Wikipedia Article - http://en.wikipedia.org/w/index. php?title=The_Protestant_Ethic_and_the_Spirit_of_Capitali (accessed March 2, 2010)

6   Lake Lambert III, *Spirituality, Inc. Religion in the Workplace* (New York: New York University Press, 2009), 99-123.

7   *Connected* Newsletter, Officer's Christian Fellowship, July 2010.

8   Richard Donkin, *The Future of Work*. (London: Palgrave Macmillan, 2010), 19.

9   Stephen Green, *Good Value: Reflections on Money, Morality, and an Uncertain World* (New York: Atlantic Monthly Press, 2010), 20-21.

10 Gary Hamel, *The Future of Management* (Massachusetts: Harvard Business Press, 2007), 169-173.

11 Harvard Business Review Article *Be a Better Leader, Have a Richer Life*. HBR April 2008.

12 Miroslav Volf, Speech titled "God At Work", Yale Divinity

School. February 2008

13   Jay W. Richards, *Money, Greed and God: Why Capitalism is the Solution and not the Problem* (New York: Harper One Publishers, 2009), 2.

14   Prov. 9:10.

15   Matthew Crawford, *Shop Class as Soulcraft: An inquiry into the value of work* (New York: The Penguin Press, 2009), 2.

16   Alain de Botton, *The Pleasures and Sorrows of Work* (New York: Pantheon Books, 2009), 29-30.

17   Buckner F. Melton, *The Quotable Founding Fathers* (Virginia: Brassey's, Inc., 2004), 157.

18   Buckner F. Melton, *The Quotable Founding Fathers* (Virginia: Brassey's, Inc., 2004), 157.

19   Gen. 2:15 English Standard Version (ESV).

20   Richard Steele, *The Religious Tradesmen* (Virginia: Sprinkle Publications, 1989 [originally written in 17th Century]), 13-14.

21   *Briefings on Talent and Leadership.* Periodical from Korn-Ferry Institute. Q3 2010 issue. 52.

22   Bill Heatley, *The Gift of Work* (Colorado Springs: NavPress Publishing, 2008), 27.

23   David Jensen, *Responsive Labor: A Theology of Work* (Kentucky: Westminster John Knox Press, 2006) 36.

24   2 Thess. 3:10.

25   2 Thess. 3:6-9.

26   Col. 3:23.

27   Darrell Cosden, *The Heavenly Good of Earthly Work* (Massachusetts: Hendrickson Publishers, 2006), 9.

28   John MacArthur, *Think Biblically! Recovering a Christian*

Worldview (Illinois: Crossway Publishing, 2003), 13.

29   Rod Gragg, *Forged in Faith: How Faith shaped the Birth of the Nation 1607-1776* (New York: Howard Publishing, 2010), 30.

30   Rod Gragg, *Forged in Faith: How Faith shaped the Birth of the Nation 1607-1776* (New York: Howard Publishing, 2010), 10-11.

31   Jon Meacham, *American Gospel* (New York: Random House Publishers, 2006), 5.

32   Steven Waldman, *Founding Faith* (New York: Random House Publishers, 2008), xi.

33   Lake Lambert III, *Spirituality, Inc. Religion in the Workplace* (New York: New York University Press, 2009), 51-78.

34   James Kennedy and Jerry Newcombe *Lord of All: Developing a Christian World and Life View* (Illinois: Crossway Publishing, 2005), 13.

35   Nancy Pearcey, *Total Truth* (Illinois: Crossway Publishing, 2004), 19.

36   1 Pet. 5:7.

37   Matt. 6:33.

38   Dallas Willard, *Knowing Christ Today* (New York: Harper One, 2009), 15.

39   Richard J. Foster, *Celebration of Discipline* (New York: Harper One Publishers, 1998), 19.

40   Matt. 6:9-13.

41   1 Thess. 5:17.

42   James 5:16.

43   John 17 (entire chapter).

44   Matt. 6:16-18.

45   Mark Lloydbottom, *Biblical Finance; Reflections on Money, Wealth, and Possessions* (London: Crown Financial Ministries, 2010), 1.

46   Isa. 34:16.

47   John 5:39.

48   Ps. 119:2-3, 9, 11, 45, 52, 66, 104-105, 114, 133, 140, 142, 160, 162, 165.

49   Matt. 6:19-21.

50   Col. 3:22-24.

51   Patrick Morley, *A Man's Guide to Work* (Chicago: Moody Publishers, 2010), 83.

52   Richard J. Foster, *Celebration of Discipline* (New York: Harper One Publishers, 1998), 64-66.

53   Phil. 4:11-12.

54   Heb. 13:5.

55   Statement from sermon at Hillsong Church London given on Palm Sunday, March 28, 2010.

56   John 13:2-15.

57   John 13:14-15.

58   Ps. 149:4.

59   Ps. 147:11.

60   Ps. 150:6.

61   Eph. 5:19-20.

62   Prov. 13:20.

63   Prov. 27:5-6.

64 Prov. 27:17.

65 Richard Donkin, *The Future of Work* (London: Palgrave Macmillan, 2010), 178.

66 Oswald J. Sanders, *Spiritual Leadership* (Chicago: Moody Publishers, 1991), 29.

67 John 16:7-11.

68 Gal. 5:22-23.

69 Note the word *fruit* is singular. Christians should be bearing all the elements of the fruit.

70 Prov. 29:18.

71 Dave Ulrich and Wendy Ulrich, *The Why of Work.*(New York: McGraw Hill Publishing, 2010), 2.

72 Joel Kurtzman, *Common Purpose* (San Francisco: Jossey-Bass Publishing, 2010).

73 Anna Bernasek, *The Economics of Integrity* (New York: Harper Collins, 2010), 14.

74 Anna Bernasek, *The Economics of Integrity* (New York: Harper Collins, 2010), 47.

75 Ps. 25:21; Ps. 26:1, 11; Prov. 11:3; Prov. 20:7.

76 Dan. 6.

77 2 Chron. 18 (entire chapter).

78 Mark 10:42-45.

79 James 1:19.

80 Prov. 13:3 (ESV)

81 Eph. 4:29.

82 James 1:20 (ESV)

83 Eph. 4:26.

84 Prov. 15:1.

85 Rev. 3:14-19.

86 Rev. Chapters 2 and 3.

87 Rev. 3:14-19.

88 Isa. 5:21; Prov. 3:5-8.

89 Prov. 9:10; 13:16; 14:8, 18; 18:15.

90 Prov. 15:5.

91 Prov. 22:3; 27:12.

92 Buckner F. Melton, *The Quotable Founding Fathers* (Virginia: Brassey's, Inc., 2004), 82.

93 Deut. 6:1-13.

94 Stu Weber, *Infinite Impact* (Illinois: Tyndale Publishers, 2007), 32.

95 John 14:26.

96 Josh. 4:1-9.

97 Stu Weber, *Infinite Impact* (Illinois: Tyndale Publishers, 2007), 58.

98 Matthew Henry, *Commentary on the Whole Bible-Volume* (Hendrickson Publishers, 1991), 15.

99 Joseph A. Michelli, *The New Gold Standard* (New York: McGraw Hill Publishing, 2008), 15.

100 Prov. 22:1.

101 Prov. 9:9.

102 Harvard Business Review July-August 2010 Double Issue, pp. 46-51.

103 Harvard Business Review July-August 2010 Double Issue, p. 51.

104 Prov. 24:10.

105 Dan. 1:8-9; 6:4-5.

106 Dan. 6:5 (ESV).

107 Prov. 27:12.

108 Esther 2:10, 21-23; 4:1-17; 8:15.

109 1 Sam. 17:1-54.

110 1 Sam. 17:31-37.

111 Acts 17:16-33.

112 Harvard Business Review interview with Howard Schultz—July/August 2010 issue.

113 Gen. 39:7-9.

114 Gen. 1:26-28.

115 John 3:16.

116 Rom. 12:17.

117 1 Thess. 5:22.

118 Prov. 1:7.

119 Col. 3:22-24.

120 Matt. 25:14-30.

121 Gen. 1:26-28.

122 Prov. 29:18.

123 William Cohen, *Drucker on Leadership* (San Francisco: Jossey-Bass, 2010), 119.

124 Jason Santamaria, Vincent Martino, and Eric Clemons, *The Marine Corps Way* (New York: McGraw-Hill, 2004).

125 Gen. 1:26.

126 Prov. 15:22 (ESV).

127 Deut. 34:9.

128 James 1:19.

129 Jim Collins, *Good to Great* (New York: Harper Business, 2001).

130 Luke 5:1-11; 6:12-16.

131 Luke 10:1-17.

132 Rev. 3:14-19.

133 Websters Dictionary On-Line 2010 (accessed September 15, 2010)

134 Josh. 5:14.

135 Josh. 5:14-15.

136 Many believe this was Christ who visited Joshua based on four reasons: the first is that he stated he was the Captain of the hosts of the Lord. Secondly, he allowed Joshua to worship him which no angel would dare let him do. Thirdly, Joshua calls him Lord. And lastly, Christ states the very ground on which Joshua is standing is holy, something only done with Divine presence.

137 *The New Encyclopedia of Christian Quotations* (Michigan: John Hunt Publishing, 2000), 477.

138 Joel Kurtzman, *Common Purpose* (San Francisco: Jossey-Bass Publishing, 2010), 15.

139 Mark Morgan; Raymond Levitt and William Malek, *Executing Your Strategy; How to break it down and get it done*

(Massachusetts: Harvard Business School Press, 2007), 1.

140 E9:10 Principle.

141 Source from internet: http://www.dhl.com/en/about_us/ company_portrait.html#history.

142 W. Chan Kim and Renee Mauborgne, *Blue Ocean Strategy* (Massachusetts: Harvard Business Press, 2005).

143 W. Chan Kim and Renee Mauborgne, *Blue Ocean Strategy* (Massachusetts: Harvard Business Press, 2005), 3.

144 W. Chan Kim and Renee Mauborgne, *Blue Ocean Strategy* (Massachusetts: Harvard Business Press, 2005), Ch. 2-6.

145 Nilofer Merchant, CEO of Rubicon Consulting, is a global high-tech industry thought leader and trusted strategic adviser for companies such as Adobe, Symantec, and VMware. She publishes and speaks frequently on strategy, innovation, and leadership. (See Rubicon Consulting website for more information.)

146 http://www.entrepreneur.com/technology/bmighty/ article196932.html (accessed October 24, 2010).

147 Prov. 15:22 (ESV).

148 Prov. 20:18 (ESV).

149 www.lean.org is a fantastic source for definitions, tools and processes around Lean Thinking including 5S.

150 Found at following web link: http://www.isixsigma.com/ index.php?option=com_k2&view=item&layout=item&id=1254 &Itemid=110 (accessed July 16, 2010).

151 John Cook, *The Book of Positive Quotations* (Minnesota: Fairview Press, 1997), 496.

152 Exod. 18.

153 Exod. 18:13-24.

154 Exod. 18:17.

155 Eccles. 9:10 (ESV).

156 Col. 3:23 (ESV).

157 A.W. Tozer, *The Pursuit of God* (Pennsylvania: Wingspread Publishing, 2007), 120-121.

158 Prov. 1:7.

159 Prov. 9:10.

160 A.W. Tozer, *The Knowledge of the Holy* (U.K.: James Clarke Publisher, 1965), 9.

161 Prov. 14:23.

162 *Newsweek* Magazine July 19, 2010 issue.

163 Article found at http://www.cnbcmagazine.com/section/ cover-story (accessed October 5, 2010).

164 Peter Drucker, *Innovation and Entrepreneurship: Practice and Principles* (New York: Harper Paperbacks, 2003).

165 *USA Today*, October 6th 2010 edition, Section C, p. 10.

166 Ps. 8:3-4.

167 Matthew Henry, *Commentary on the Whole Bible-Volume 3* (Hendrickson Publishers, 1991), 217.

168 Ps. 139:14.

169 Ravi Zacharias, *Recapture the Wonder* (Tennessee: Integrity Publishing, 2003),165.

170 Elizabeth Barrett Browning, *Aurora Leigh,* book 7, lines 821-24.

171 Ravi Zacharias, *Recapture the Wonder* (Tennessee: Integrity

Publishing, 2003), 164.

172 *The New Encyclopedia of Christian Quotations* (Michigan: John Hunt Publishing, 2000), 1139.

173 A.W. Tozer (edited by James Snyder), *The Purpose of Man* (California: Regal Publishers, 2009), 52.

174 James 5:16.

175 Peter Senge, *The Necessary Revolution* (New York: Double Day Publishers, 2008), 14-18.

176 Gen. 1:27.

177 Job 41:11.

178 Ps. 24:1.

179 Deut. 10:14.

180 1 Cor. 10:26.

181 Col. 1:16-17.

182 Deut. 11:12.

183 Matt. 6:25-34.

184 Gen. 1:28.

185 John MacArthur, *The MacArthur Bible Commentary* (Tennessee: Thomas Nelson Publishers, 2005), 11.

186 Peter Senge, *The Necessary Revolution* (New York: Double Day Publishers, 2008).

187 http://en.wikipedia.org/wiki/Leadership_in_Energy_and_Environmental_Design (accessed December 6, 2010).

188 http://www.elyrics.net/read/a/alabama-lyrics/pass-it-on-down-lyrics.html (accessed December 16, 2010).

189 Ps. 19:14.

190 Ps. 46:10.

191 Prov. 3:5-6.

192 I have been privileged to travel to all of these countries, many on several occasions where I have had the opportunity to speak with business leaders, university students and ministry leaders and have witnessed these factors in literally hundreds of situations from meetings, documents, speaking engagements, 1:1's, and research.

193 Any web-search of productivity studies will bring the reader large amounts of data to support this.

194 Eph. 5:16.

195 Eccles. 3:1-8.

196 Matthew Henry, *Commentary on the Whole Bible-Volume 3* (Hendrickson Publishers, 1991), 819.

197 Laura Vanderkam, *168 Hours: You have More Time than You Think* (New York: Penguin Group, 2010).

198 Stephen Covey, A. Roger Merrill, Rebecca R. Merrill, *First Things First: To Live, to Love, to Learn, to Leave a Legacy* (New York: Simon and Schuster, 1994).

199 Phil. 4:11-12.

200 Laura Vanderkam, *168 Hours: You have More Time than You Think* (New York: Penguin Group, 2010).

201 Eccles. 9:10.

202 Hal Moore, *A Tender Warrior: 5 Leadership Letters to America* (Illinois: Simple Truths Publishers, 2009), 118.

203 Charles H. Spurgeon and Alistair Begg (Editor), *Evening by Evening* (Illinois: Crossway Publishers, 2007), 191.

204 Heb. 4:12.

205   U.S. Religious Knowledge Survey–September 2010
      conducted by Pew Forum on Religion & Public Life.

206   Matt. 6:33.

Intermedia Publishing Group

Publishing That Works For You

Do you need a speaker?

Do you want Gary Blackard to speak to your group or event? Then contact Larry Davis at: (623) 337-8710 or email: ldavis@intermediapr.com or use the contact form at: www.intermediapr.com.

Whether you want to purchase bulk copies of *Relevance in the Workplace* or buy another book for a friend, get it now at: www.imprbooks.com.

If you have a book that you would like to publish, contact Terry Whalin, Publisher, at Intermedia Publishing Group, (623) 337-8710 or email: twhalin@intermediapub.com or use the contact form at: www.intermediapub.com.